THE MANY FACETS OF STEPHEN KING

MORE WILDSIDE CLASSICS

Dacobra, or The White Priests of Ahriman, by Harris Burland
The Nabob, by Alphonse Daudet
Out of the Wreck, by Captain A. E. Dingle
The Elm-Tree on the Mall, by Anatole France
The Lance of Kanana, by Harry W. French
Amazon Nights, by Arthur O. Friel
Caught in the Net, by Emile Gaboriau
The Gentle Grafter, by O. Henry
Raffles, by E. W. Hornung
Gates of Empire, by Robert E. Howard
Tom Brown's School Days, by Thomas Hughes
The Opium Ship, by H. Bedford Jones
The Miracles of Antichrist, by Selma Lagerlof
Arsène Lupin, by Maurice LeBlanc
A Phantom Lover, by Vernon Lee
The Iron Heel, by Jack London
The Witness for the Defence, by A.E.W. Mason
The Spider Strain and Other Tales, by Johnston McCulley
Tales of Thubway Tham, by Johnston McCulley
The Prince of Graustark, by George McCutcheon
Bull-Dog Drummond, by Cyril McNeile
The Moon Pool, by A. Merritt
The Red House Mystery, by A. A. Milne
Blix, by Frank Norris
Wings over Tomorrow, by Philip Francis Nowlan
The Devil's Paw, by E. Phillips Oppenheim
Satan's Daughter and Other Tales, by E. Hoffmann Price
The Insidious Dr. Fu Manchu, by Sax Rohmer
Mauprat, by George Sand
The Slayer and Other Tales, by H. de Vere Stacpoole
Penrod (Gordon Grant Illustrated Edition), by Booth Tarkington
The Gilded Age, by Mark Twain
The Blockade Runners, by Jules Verne
The Gadfly, by E.L. Voynich

Please see www.wildsidepress.com for a complete list!

THE MANY FACETS OF STEPHEN KING

by
MICHAEL R. COLLINGS

WILDSIDE PRESS

THE MANY FACETS OF STEPHEN KING

This edition published in 2006 by Wildside Press, LLC.
www.wildsidepress.com

Table of Contents

As a composition instructor, I frequently approach the word _facet_ with emotions akin to dread. Too many student writers use it as an easy substitute for _thing_--a word included to impress more than to express. The word recurs in phrases such as "another facet of the educational process" or "another facet of socialization," without regard for the fact that processes (or most _-tion_ nouns for that matter) simply do not have facets; the word implies "sides" or "aspects" (another dangerously vague word), characteristics noticeably lacking from most generalizations. As a result, it sometimes seems the easiest solution simply to ban the word from composition.

The easiest, yes--but not the fairest.

As with so many other misused words, _facets_ carries valuable meaning when used appropriately. In architecture, in anatomy, in zoology, the word communicates specific ideas; more commonly, it refers to the small polished plane surfaces of cut gems--a concrete reference for a word usually approached as an abstraction.

By calling this study _The Many Facets of Stephen King_, I urge readers to aproach King from multiple directions, just as he approaches his craft from multiple directions. There is in fact much more to Stephen King than his reputation as "King of Horror" suggests. When one considers the immense range of his novels, short fiction, criticism, screenplays, and poetry, it becomes clear that there are indeed many _facets_ to the man, the artist, the critic, and the social phenomenon.

This is the point where many studies of King have faltered. Most critical approaches emphasize chronology. Peter M. Gareffa's sketch in _Contemporary Authors_, for example, works through King's publications in sequence: several brief paragraphs devoted to each novel (excepting the Bachman books, of course), with a brief concluding note that several novels have been adapted as films. The 1981 entry in _Current Biography Yearbook_ follows the same pattern: a chronological overview of

1

King's life and publications, concluding with a number of concise critical assessments.

Two subsequent (and more extensive) studies also follow this pattern. Douglas Winter's Stephen King (Starmont, 1982; revised as Stephen King: The Art of Darkness, NAL, 1984) is organized around King's chronological development, as is James Van Hise's Enterprise Incidents Presents Stephen King. Even my own recent contributions to King scholarship and criticism, Stephen King as Richard Bachman (Starmont, 1985) and The Shorter Works of Stephen King (with David Engebretson; Starmont, 1985) adhere to chronological ordering.

It seems time, then, for another approach, an extension of the varied thematic treatments in Tim Underwood and Chuck Miller's Fear Itself: The Horror Fiction of Stephen King (1982, 1984). In The Many Facets, I propose to break from the chronology of King's life and career and focus instead on the "facets" of his work--on the multiple perspectives of "reality" King has chosen to explore. As a result, works published ten or fifteen years apart will share (however uneasily on the surface) the same chapters: 'Salem's Lot with Pet Sematary, or Carrie with "The Reach."

The purpose behind such an arrangement is not merely iconoclastic, however; there are functional reasons for de-emphasizing a dependence on chronology. Many of King's works were published long after they were completed in manuscript--the Bachman novels are the best examples, but stories such as "The Raft" (originally written in 1968, revised and published in 1982) illustrate the same difficulty. In addition, many of the later novels seem outgrowths of images or kernel ideas King toyed with during college.

And finally, King frequently works on several projects simultaneously--during the years he has been writing It (roughly 1979-1986), he published The Long Walk, Roadwork, The Running Man, Christine, Pet Sematary, Danse Macabre, The Dead Zone, Firestarter, Cujo, portions of The Dark Tower, Different Seasons, The Talisman, The Eyes of the Dragon, Cycle of the Werewolf, several stories collected in Skeleton Crew, and the screenplays for Creepshow and Cat's Eye, as well as working on other projects currently in various stages of completion. To say that It should be isolated from

2

what King was doing during those years and considered only as a novel published in 1986 or 1987 would lessen the work.

The Many Facets of Stephen King also has another purpose. Implicit in virtually every study of King is the sense that he epitomizes horror fiction. There are certainly strong and sufficient reasons for such an assumption. He is, as one writer notes, the only American ever to have three novels on the bestsellers lists simultaneously: Firestarter, The Dead Zone, and The Shining in 1980. All three are to some extent "horror" novels, yet to lump these three together under one classification is to ignore critical differences among them. If we then place 'Salem's Lot next to The Talisman, or Rage against Christine, we discover that in spite of King's reputation, there is more in his novels than merely "accounts of man-eating rats, gigantic worms, vampires, murder, revenge, and bloodletting" (Gareffa 334).

True, there are monsters; "The Mist" seems a culmination of King's fascination with things from beyond our understanding. But there is also the unnervingly "real" world of Johnny Smith in The Dead Zone.

> Though the characters are not complex, for the most part, they breathe a warmth and love of life it is easy to relate to. By creating a world so very close to our own existence, then disturbing it with a frightening supposition, King offers a horror no seven-foot green monster or fanged stalker ever can. After all, horror we can place in an isolation booth is one thing. Horror let loose in the real world in quite another. (Gareffa 335)

In Stephen King's writing, we explore many "facets" of horror as they glint from widely divergent perspectives. King's writing is not straight-line in the sense that he went through a "mainstream phase," a separate "horror phase," or a distinct "epic-fantasy quest" phase. Instead, his forms and themes intertwine, reflecting each other, glittering like the continuous movement of light around a brilliantly set gem-stone.

3

Thus, <u>The Many Facets of Stephen King</u>, concentrating on works not included in <u>Stephen King as Richard Bachman</u> or <u>The Shorter Works of Stephen King</u>.

This study, like the two preceding it, owes much to earlier writers: Douglas Winter; Tim Underwood, Chuck Miller, and the contributors to <u>Fear Itself</u>; James Van Hise; and King's many reviewers and interviewers. In addition, my debt to Stephanie Leonard and <u>Castle Rock</u>, already mentioned in the two earlier studies, continues unabated. Barbara Bolan remains a mainstay and a support, locating hard-to-find materials and opening lines of communication with book dealers and collectors. Excellences in this study can frequently be traced back to these people; weaknesses are, I fear, my own.

My thanks also to Stephen King. It is both exciting and intimidating to study living authors--they have the disconcerting habit of publishing new works before the criticism even reaches the readers. But that is the stuff of literature; it merely enhances the challenge. Working this intensely with King has given me new insight into the nature of horror fiction, into the functions and forms of literature, and into contemporary trends . . . and, lest it be overlooked, enormous enjoyment.

Michael R. Collings
Thousand Oaks CA

August 1985

ABBREVIATIONS

Art   Stephen King: The Art of Darkness, by
        Douglas E. Winter (NAL, 1984)
CBY   Current Biography Yearbook, 1981
CR   Castle Rock: The Stephen King Newsletter
Cycle   Cycle of the Werewolf (1981)
DM   Danse Macabre (1981)
DS   Different Seasons (1982)
DSK   Discovering Stephen King, ed. Darrell
        Schweitzer (Starmont 1985)
DT   The Dark Tower: The Gunslinger (1982)
DZ   The Dead Zone (1979)
ED   The Eyes of the Dragon (1984)
FI   Fear Itself, ed. Tim Underwood and Chuck
        Miller (Underwood-Miller, 1982; NAL,
        1984)
FSF   The Magazine of Fantasy and Science Fiction
"GT"   "King's Garbage Truck"
KC   King's Crypt (Newsletter)
LW   The Long Walk ("Bachman," 1979)
NS   Night Shift (1978)
PS   Pet Sematary (1983)
RG/SK   Reader's Guide to Stephen King, by Douglas
        E. Winter (Starmont, 1982)
RM   The Running Man ("Bachman," 1982)
RW   Roadwork ("Bachman," 1981)
SC   Skeleton Crew (1985)
SK/RB   Stephen King as Richard Bachman by Michael
        R. Collings (Starmont, 1985)
SL   'Salem's Lot (1975)
SW   The Shorter Works of Stephen King, by
        Michael R. Collings and David A.
        Engebretson (Starmont, 1985)

Chapter I

Canon and Critical Overview

    While it may seem self-contradictory, in
light of my "Foreword," to begin The Many Facets
of Stephen King with a chronology, such information clarifies the sequence of King's works and
their implicit relationships. Chronology in and
of itself is at best pedestrian; as a guide to
when certain works appeared--particularly in a
study which has consciously refrained from a continuing sense of chronological sequence--it may
help avoid potential confusion.
    And if nothing else, a chronological listing
clearly demonstrates King's consistent prolif-
icacy.

1948-1956: King was born in Portland, Maine, on
    September 21, the second child in his family.
    His father, a merchant sailor named Donald
    King, left a year later; King never saw him
    again. His mother, Nellie Ruth (Pillsbury)
    King, supported her two sons through a variety
    of jobs, including working in a laundry (a
    motif that would recur repeatedly in King's
    prose). During this period, King lived for
    several years in Fort Wayne, Indiana, and
    Stratford, Connecticut. He saw the first
    motion picture he remembers (The Creature from
    the Black Lagoon) and began writing short
    stories.
1957: Russia successfully orbited its Sputnik sat-
    ellite. King recalls the fear he felt at that
    moment, his sense of impending doom. America
    had been the "good guys," the front runner in
    the space race. Suddenly, for King at least,
    "it was the end of the sweet dream . . . and
    the beginning of the nightmare" (DM 24).
1958: King's family moved to Durham, Maine, where
    Nellie King began caring for her parents, an
    experience King later transformed into the hor-

ror story "Gramma."

1959-1962: The discovery of a collection of paperback books his father had left behind stimulated King's interest in science fiction and
adventure. He worked even more seriously on
his own writing, especially after finding out
that Donald King had unsuccessfully submitted
horror stories to such magazines as <u>Bluebook</u>
and <u>Argosy</u> (<u>CBY</u> 253).

1963-1966: King attended the Lisbon Falls high
school. Although he participated in sports and
played rhythm guitar for a rock 'n roll band
(providing the basis for his later dedication
to rock 'n' roll, both in his life and in his
fiction), he also continued writing, winning a
prize in an essay contest sponsored by a scho-
lastic magazine.

1964: King completed "The Star Invaders," the only
surviving example of his early self-published
booklets. An uneasy attempt at science fiction, it modulates into a subtle exploration of
horror under the guise of science fiction.

1965: "I Was a Teenage Grave Robber," King's first
published story, appeared in a fanzine; it was
later reprinted as "In a Half-world of Terror."

1966: As a freshman at the University of Maine at
Orono, King began working toward an English
degree. He also wrote the first half of a
novel-length project that would result seven
years later in <u>Rage.</u> "I didn't rewrite it
much," King has noted. "It still has a quirky
sophomore quality to it" (Brown, C4).

1967: "The Glass Floor," King's first professional
sale, appeared in <u>Startling Mystery Stories</u>,
Fall 1967. During that year (1966-1967), he
also completed the manuscript for <u>The Long
Walk</u>, the second Bachman novel, published in
1979.

1968: While still at UMO, King began <u>Sword in the
Darkness</u>, a race-riot novel King later referred
to as "just terrible" (Also called <u>Babylon
Here</u>, the ms. was completed in 1969). In the
spring and fall issues of <u>Ubris</u>, the UMO
literary magazine, he published "Cain Rose Up,"
"Here There Be Tygers," the original version of
"Strawberry Spring," and a poem, "Harrison
State Park '68."

1969: In February, King began writing a weekly

column for <u>The Maine Campus</u>, "King´s Garbage Truck," which would continue until his graduation; the final column appeared in May, 1970. On 11 July 1969, he responded to the moon-walk, writing of a dream of madness and fear, of a

> huge, tideless wind [that] has swept down on them and their puny ship, a cyclopean gale from no place that is sweeping them off their neatly computerized orbit and into the gaping germless map of deep space itself.

* Publications: "The Reaper´s Image," his second professional sale, again in <u>Startling Mystery Stories</u>; "Night Surf," "Stud City" (later incorporated into "The Body"), and a poem, "The Dark Man," all in <u>Ubris</u>.
1970: King graduated from UMO with a degree in English. He also completed a novel, <u>Blaze</u>, a "reworking of Steinbeck´s <u>Of Mice and Men</u>, and kind of a ghost story" (Letter 3 August 1985).
* Publications: "Graveyard Shift," his first sale to <u>Cavalier</u>, one of his main markets for several years; "It Grows on You"; "Slade," serialized in <u>The Maine Campus</u> from 11 June to 6 August 1970.
1971: King married Tabitha Spruce, whom he had met while working in the library at UMO. Writing in "one feverish weekend" (Brown, C4), he completed <u>The Running Man</u>, published in 1981 as the fourth Bachman novel. He also finished the ms. for <u>Rage</u> and submitted the novel as <u>Getting It On</u> to Doubleday in late 1971 or early 1972. He began teaching English at Hampden Academy, a position he held for two years.
* Publications: "The Blue Air Compressor" and an untitled poem in <u>Onan</u>; "I Am the Doorway."
1972: After finishing his fourth novel in manuscript, King started a short story, "Carrie"; it later outgrew its form and developed into his first novel sale.
* Publications: "Battleground"; "The Fifth Quarter," published under King´s first pseudonym, John Swithen; "The Mangler"; "Suffer the Little Children."
1973: Doubleday purchased <u>Carrie</u>, allowing King to quit teaching and write full time. He also

began a novel, <u>Second Coming</u>, which evolved
into ´Salem´s Lot. His mother died of cancer
before <u>Carrie</u>´s release; her death formed the
central image for "The Woman in the Room."
* Publications: "The Boogeyman"; "Gray Matter";
"Trucks."
1974: King completed <u>´Salem´s Lot</u> and <u>Roadwork</u>,
published seven years later as the third Bach-
man novel, and began <u>The Stand</u> and <u>The Shining</u>
while he was living in Boulder, Colorado.
* Publications: <u>Carrie</u>; "Sometimes They Come
Back"; the revised "Night Surf," with its
thematic connections to <u>The Stand</u>.
1975: After returning to Maine, King completed the
first draft of <u>The Stand</u>.
* Publications: <u>´Salem´s Lot</u>; "It Grows on You";
"The Lawnmower Man"; "The Revenge of Lard Ass
Hogan" (incorporated into "The Body"); the
revised "Strawberry Spring," with additions
that enhance it as a study of guilt and hidden
terror.
1976: Brian de Palma´s film version of <u>Carrie</u> was
released, assuring King´s reputation; "The
movie made the book," King has noted, "and the
book made me" (Lawson).
* Publications: "I Know What You Need"; "The
Ledge"; "Weeds."
* Film: De Palma´s <u>Carrie.</u>
1977: Within one year, King completed initial
drafts of three novels: <u>The Dead Zone</u>, <u>Fire-
starter</u>, and <u>Cujo</u>. He traveled to England,
where he met Peter Straub and began a friend-
ship that would lead to <u>The Talisman</u>.
* Publications: <u>The Shining</u>; <u>Rage</u>; "The Cat from
Hell"; "Children of the Corn"; "The Man Who
Loved Flowers"; "One for the Road," a return
visit to ´Salem´s Lot.
1978: During a year as Writer-in-Residence at UMO,
King delivered a series of lectures that
evolved into <u>Danse Macabre</u>. He also acted as
judge for the 1977 World Fantasy Awards.
* Publications: <u>The Stand</u>; <u>Night Shift</u> (including
"Jerusalem´s Lot", "The Last Rung on the Lad-
der", "Quitters, Inc.," and "The Woman in the
Room"); "Man With a Belly"; "The Night of the
Tiger"; "Nona."
1979: As in 1977, King again drafted three books
(<u>Christine</u>, <u>Pet Sematary</u>, and <u>Danse Macabre</u>) as

well as the screeenplay for <u>Creepshow</u>. A guest
of honor at the World Fantasy Convention, he
also received World Fantasy Award nominations
for <u>The Stand</u> and <u>Night Shift</u>.
* Publications: <u>The Dead Zone</u>; <u>The Long Walk</u>
  (Bachman); "The Crate."
* Film: <u>'Salem's Lot</u>, a television mini-series
  directed by Tobe Hooper.
1980: King moved to Bangor, Maine, after pur-
  chasing an old Victorian mansion. He completed
  the first draft of his "magnum opus," <u>IT</u>,
  scheduled for publication in 1986 or 1987. He
  became the first American to have three books
  on the bestsellers lists simultaneously: <u>Fire-
  starter</u>, <u>The Dead Zone</u>, and <u>The Shining</u>. He
  also made his film debut with an appearance in
  George Romero's <u>Knightriders.</u>
* Publications: <u>Firestarter</u>; "The Mist"; "Big
  Wheels: A Tale of the Laundry Game"; "Crouch
  End"; "The Gunslinger"; "The Monkey"; "The Way
  Station"; "The Wedding Gig."
* Film: Stanley Kubrick's <u>The Shining</u>.
1981: The University of Maine acknowledged King's
  achievements with a Career Alumni Award; with
  his multiple nominations for World Fantasy
  Awards and Nebula Awards, as well as his
  receiving a special British Fantasy Award, the
  Alumni award signals King's growing reputation.
* Publications: <u>Cujo</u>; <u>Roadwork</u> (Bachman); <u>Danse
  Macabre</u> (non-fiction); "The Bird and the Album"
  (an excerpt from <u>IT</u>); "Do the Dead Sing?"; "The
  Gunslinger and the Dark Man"; "The Jaunt"; "The
  Man Who Would Not Shake Hands"; "The Oracle and
  the Mountain"; "The Slow Mutants."
1982: King began two novels: <u>The Talisman</u>, with
  Peter Straub; and <u>The Cannibals</u>. He also completed the final Bachman novel, <u>Thinner</u>, and
  received a number of awards, including a Hugo
  for <u>Danse Macabre</u>, the British Fantasy Award
  for <u>Cujo</u>, and the World Fantasy Award for "Do
  the Dead Sing?" Douglas Winter published the
  first full-scale critical study of King, <u>The
  Reader's Guide to Stephen King</u> for Starmont
  House, and Tim Underwood and Chuck Miller published their collection of criticism, <u>Fear Itself: The Horror Fiction of Stephen King</u>.
* Publications: <u>The Dark Tower: The Gunslinger</u>;
  <u>Different Seasons</u> ("Rita Hayworth and Shawshank

Redemption," "Apt Pupil," "The Body," and "The Breathing Method"); <u>Creepshow</u> ("Father´s Day"; "The Lonesome Death of Jordy Verrill," an adaptation of "Weeds" starring King as Jordy Verrill; "The Crate"; "Something to Tide You Over"; and "They´re Creeping Up on You"); <u>The Running Man</u> (Bachman); "Before the Play"; "The Plant" Part 1; "The Raft"; "Skybar"; "Survivor Type."
* Film: George Romero´s <u>Creepshow</u>, in which King participated as both writer and actor.
1983: Again, King completed first drafts for three novels (<u>The Talisman</u>; <u>The Tommyknockers</u>; and <u>The Napkins</u>, published as <u>The Eyes of the Dragon</u>), and a screenplay, <u>Cat´s Eye</u>.
* Publications: <u>Christine</u>; <u>Pet Sematary</u>; <u>Cycle of the Werewolf</u>; "The Plant," Part 2; "Uncle Otto´s Truck"; "The Word Processor."
* Films: Lewis Teague´s <u>Cujo</u>; David Cronenberg´s <u>The Dead Zone</u>; John Carpenter´s <u>Christine</u>.
1984: Winter´s <u>Stephen King: The Art of Darkness</u> was published through NAL.
* Publications: <u>The Talisman</u> (with Peter Straub); <u>The Eyes of the Dragon</u>, in a limited edition of 1250 copies; <u>Thinner</u>, the final Bachman novel and the one that forced King to acknowledge the pseudonym; "The Ballad of the Flexible Bullet"; "Gramma"; "Mrs. Todd´s Shortcut"; "The Revelations of ´Becka Paulson."
* Films: "The Word Processor of the Gods," produced for the television series <u>Tales from the Darkside</u>; student productions of <u>The Boogeyman</u> and <u>The Woman in the Room</u>.
1985: In January, Stephanie Leonard, King´s secretary, began publishing <u>Castle Rock: The Stephen King Newsletter</u> as an official source of information about King. In March, he acknowledged the "Bachman" pseudonym; the subsequent interest in finding more "hidden" novels by Stephen King resulted in a review-hoax falsely linking King to a non-existent pornographic novel. An unexpurgated version of <u>The Stand</u> was scheduled for later 1985, but the project stalled over contractual problems; an omnibus edition of the first four Bachman novels (<u>Rage</u>, <u>The Long Walk</u>, <u>Roadwork</u>, and <u>The Running Man</u>) is scheduled from NAL in late 1985. Starmont House began publishing its series of critical studies.

* Publications: <u>Skeleton Crew</u> (including "Paranoid: A Chant" [poem], "For Owen" [poem], and
  "Morning Deliveries [Milkman #1]"); the trade
  edition of <u>Cycle of the Werewolf</u>; "Beachworld";
  "Dolan´s Cadillac," serialized in <u>CR</u>.
* Films: <u>Cat´s Eye</u>, written by King and directed
  by Lewis Teague. <u>Silver Bullet</u> (based on <u>Cycle
  of the Werewolf</u>), <u>Maximum Overdrive</u> (based on
  "Trucks"), <u>The Body</u>, <u>The Stand</u>, <u>Pet Sematary</u>,
  and a television version of "Gramma" are all in
  various stages of production. Two of the
  Bachman novels are also scheduled for production, as is a musical version of <u>Carrie</u>.
1986-1987: As a result of a multi-million dollar
  contract, King will publish four novels in
  fourteen months: <u>IT</u>, <u>The Eyes of the Dragon</u>
  (trade edition); <u>Misery</u>, and <u>The Tommyknockers</u>.

As prolific and popular as King is, many
critics (particularly "mainstream" critics) have
dealt harshly with him. His writing, they say,
is marred by prolixity; by syntactic confusion; by
"pseudoscientific hokum" (Demarest); by a flat,
inelegant, and heavy-handed style; and by uninten-
tional humor. Elizabeth Hall and Jan Belon Shaw
objected to the blood and violence in <u>Carrie</u>;
Walter Bobbie commented on the unnecessary elonga-
tion" of ´Salem´s Lot; Richard Lingman noted that
King lacks the "sly craftsmanship" of Ira Levin
and the "narrative strength" of Thomas Tryon (Gareffa 334). Christopher Lehmann-Haupt referred to
<u>Cujo</u> as cruel and disturbing (Gareffa 254); when
asking rhetorically if <u>Cujo</u> was a good novel, Jean
Strouse answered simply, "Of course not." Leslie
Fiedler called King the "master of horror schlock"
(9), while Paul Gray discussed him extensively as
the "master of postliterate prose."
   The problem is that King, like his forebears in
horror fiction, Edgar Allan Poe and H. P. Lovecraft, "has not been taken very seriously, if at
all, by the critical establishment" (Slung 147),
in King´s case both because of his chosen genre
and because of his enormous commercial success
within it. Even when trying to separate King from
the genre, Charles de Lint paradoxically emphasizes King´s identification with horror by writing
that <u>ED</u> proves "once and for all that while he can
deliver the shocks, he doesn´t need them to be one

13

of America´s premier story tellers."

That is in fact the crux of the matter. King may lapse into stylistic infelicities; Straub noted one particular case in "Meeting Stevie" (FI 8-9). He is on occasion (and by his own admission) afflicted with "literary elephantiasis" (DS 508). Yet, as de Lint implies and a number of other critics have admitted, ultimately those technical problems fade and the story takes over. In many cases, the story is based on terror or horror; yet invariably, beneath the horror lies an extraordinary talent for the tale well told.

It is this talent that I propose to explore in The Many Facets of Stephen King.

Chapter II

THE SEARCH FOR A FORM:
EARLY WRITINGS

In a recent interview, King was asked why he
wrote. "You don´t do it for money," he said,

> don´t think of it in terms of hourly
> wage, yearly wage, even lifetime wage
> . . . . In the end you don´t even do it
> for love. . . . You do it because to not
> do it is suicide. (Foltz 62)

For King, writing as compulsion (Foltz refers to
his "obsessive scribbling") has been virtually a
life-long experience--and for most of that time,
he has worked within what could loosely be defined
as the "fantastic": science fiction, fantasy, dark
fantasy, and supernatural horror. The results of
his dedication/compulsion/obsession include:

* Over 50,000,000 books in print; earnings in
  excess of $20,000,000; and a publishing con-
  tract which specifies that rights to two new
  books revert to King in fifteen years;

* Films (completed or in production) of almost
  all of his novels, a number of short stories,
  and several original screenplays;

* And the undisputed reputation as the King of
  Modern Horror or, in Foltz´ phrasing, the
  "Titan of Terror" (62).

The accomplishments did not come easily,
however. King began writing early, around the age
of seven, and has continued to do so--at the rate
of 1500-2000 words a day, excluding Christmas, the
Fourth of July, and September 21 (his birthday).

15

In addition, most of his early attempts and his earliest publications clearly show his interest in and command of a chosen genre: horror.

This interest, however, was neither all-encompassing nor absolute. King also tried his hand at a number of other forms and genres. The "Afterword" to Different Seasons reproduces an enlightening conversation between King and his editor at Doubleday, Bill Thompson. King had sent Thompson two manuscripts as possibilities to follow the success of Carrie. The first, according to the "Afterword," was Blaze, "a melodrama about a huge, almost retarded criminal who kidnaps a baby, planning to ransom it back to the child's rich parents . . . and then falls in love with the child instead" (519); in a recent letter, however, King identified the second manuscript as Roadwork, later published as the fourth Bachman novel--presumably the reference to Blaze was an attempt at discrediting any rumors then circulating that Stephen King was Richard Bachman (Letter, 3 August 1985). The other manuscript, then titled Second Coming, while equally melodramatic, was about vampires coming to a New England town.

Thompson opted for the second, although with an odd sense of reluctance. Pushed for an explanation, he said that he feared King would be typed--as a horror writer. The fear deepened with the third novel, The Shining, about a haunted hotel. But by that time, King had thought the question through, deciding that belonging to a group that included H.P. Lovecraft, Clark Ashton Smith, Frank Belknap Long, Fritz Leiber, Robert Bloch, Richard Matheson, and Shirley Jackson was itself a worthwhile goal.

He had committed himself to horror, a decision he has never regretted.

Yet, some years later, when Different Seasons appeared and demonstrated that King could write equally strongly outside of horror, reactions were mixed. Some readers were pleased to see that King could move in other directions; others ignored the collection because it was not horror.

A look into King's background, however, might have lessened the extremity of both of those viewpoints. Although primarily known for his horror fantasies, King has written mainstream fiction, including three of the Bachman novels, three

16

stories in DS, several in Night Shift, and a number of early uncollected stories. In addition, he has explored other sub-genres, often with remarkable success. As de Lint noted about ED, King does not need the shocks and the horrors to establish his power as a story-teller.

In fact, this sense of exploration begins early in his career. The first story he wrote has long since disappeared, but he recalls it as a science-fiction tale about a dinosaur come to life and subsequently overcome by its allergy to leather (Art 17; SW 7-8). Later, he refined his interest in science fiction, producing "The Star Invaders" (1964), a self-published pamphlet that represents King's earliest extant writing. The story is highly derivative, its plot a re-working of the space-ships-versus-earthlings pattern that figures so prominently in the films King enjoyed during the late 1950s--specifically Earth vs. the Flying Saucers. In Danse Macabre, King refers to the "pulpy-invaders-from-space storyline" of the film (26), an equally accurate description of his own story. Since "The Star Invaders" is discussed fully in the first chapter of SW (10-12), it would be redundant here to repeat verbatim its strengths and weaknesses--except to stress its generic indecisiveness. While the story is overtly modeled on science fiction, it undergoes the same transformation as many of the films that influenced (and inspired) it. While beginning within a science-fictional framework, it edges into horror. It provides images of fear and terror King would later develop more fully in works such as Carrie and "The Raft." Even his latest foray into science fiction--"Beachworld," first published in 1985 and collected in SC the same year--shows the same impulse. While ostensibly science fiction in setting and characterization, it ultimately reveals itself as horror in disguise.

King's early commitment to horror develops even more fully in his two subsequent stories: "I Was a Teenage Grave Robber" (1965), his first published story; and "The Glass Floor" (1967), his first professional sale. In each, King follows traditional forms and directions, producing stories at once workmanlike and conventional. Neither suggests the power he would develop over the next few years. And both lie safely within

17

the niche of traditional horror fiction. "I Was a Teenage Grave Robber" employs the stock figures of the mad scientist, his delectable young daughter, and the innocent youth who must save her from the horrors her own father has created--the stuff of innumerable "B" movies.

"The Glass Floor," while far beyond the workaday prose of "The Star Invader" and "Teenage Grave Robber," is still derivative, depending upon Poe and Lovecraft for its situational and atmospheric horror. It demonstrates King's interest in characterization, but only marginally. And the focus of horror, the mirrored floor, remains curiously undeveloped, as do the motivations that underlie the story: the reason behind Charles Wharton's visit to the hideous old mansion is as unsatisfying as Anthony Reynard's letting his wife Janine into a room already infamous for mysterious happenings. While the story engages the reader's interest on several levels, it too seems best categorized as conventional horror.

Within the next two years, however, King's writing underwent a radical change, due in part to his exposure to wider varieties of writing in the course of earning an English degree at the University of Maine. His interest in supernatural horror remained, of course, and resulted in his second published story, "The Reaper's Image" (1969; SC 1985), a much stronger, more independent piece of atmospheric horror than King had yet produced. While still drawing on Poe and Lovecraft, it illustrates King's growing command of the form and of literary structures and devices in general. He carefully weaves critical flashbacks into the texture of the story; his characterizations are more self-consistent; and he allows the mystery of the DeIver mirror to develop its own power rather than imposing a mystery upon the characters, as he had done in "The Glass Floor."

Even more importantly, however, King also began writing and publishing stories that moved away from strict supernatural horror. "Cain Rose Up" (1968; SC 1985), written shortly after King had worked through what would become the first Bachman novel, Rage, has its own share of horror. The insane sniper, hidden in an upper room and randomly firing at passersby has become part of

18

the arsenal of terrifying images society shares.
Yet in his first version, King de-emphasized the
implicit horror of the visual images. Garrish
(the name immediately suggests Raymond Garraty of
The Long Walk) fires at a girl and blows her head
off. "Her mother went on smiling for a moment,"
King continues in the Ubris version:

> . . . then her hand went up to her mouth,
> and she screamed. Garrish could hear her
> all the way up where he was--a high, thin
> faraway sound, as if the scream were
> coming over a telephone wire. She looked
> very close in the telescopic sight. Gar-
> rish blew her head off, and the man who
> had been loading the suitcases started to
> run. (34)

King emphasizes the action, describing it neutrally, in a voice almost clinically detached and
immediate. In the 1985 revision, he alters the
text to capitalize on visual horror:

> Her mother went on smiling for a mo-
> ment, and then her hand went to her
> mouth. She screamed through her hand.
> Garrish shot through it. Hand and head
> disappeared in a red spray. The man who
> had been loading the suitcases broke into
> a lumbering run. (SC 179)

Similarly, a few paragraphs later, the original
version reads simply that Garrish "shot Quinn,
missed the head, got the shoulder, and had to
shoot him again" (35). In SC, King expands the
incident, coupling the sense of mindless violence
with a parody of a child's prayer:

> "Good drink, good meat, good God,
> let´s eat!" Garrish exclaimed, and shot
> at Quinn. He pulled instead of squeezing
> and the shot went wide. Quinn was run-
> ning. No problem. The second shot took
> Quinn in the neck and he flew maybe twen-
> ty feet. (179)

In each instance, and elsewhere in "Cain Rose Up,"
what was initially a starkly brutal study of a

19

student subjected to unendurable pressure has been transformed into an image of graphic violence and visual horror.

"Strawberry Spring" (1968; NS 1978) underwent a similar transformation. What had originally appeared as a psychological study--but without any overtly horrific overtones--later becomes a powerful study of repression and terror. In the Ubris original, there is no suggestion that the narrator is connected with the series of vicious murders other than as observer. The story depends again upon tone and atmosphere for its power; the inexplicable and frighteningly brutal murders differ little from what we are used to seeing in headlines and on the evening news. The NS version, on the other hand, consciously intrudes an element of horror--the narrator fears that he may himself be the murderer. He does not remember . . . quite, and he fears to find out. Both stories are powerful, but in different directions. The revision moves "Strawberry Spring" closer to what King is best known for; the original stands well within mainstream fiction.

"Night Surf" (1969; NS 1978), important as an image kernel for The Stand, follows a similar pattern. The original version begins neutrally: "After the guy was dead and the fire was down to coals, we went back to the beach" (Ubris 6). For its appearance in NS, King adds graphic, sensory horror: "After the guy was dead and the smell of his burning flesh was off the air, we all went back down to the beach" (52). Again, the revisions emphasize something inherently grisly but understated in the original.

A final story published in Ubris, "Stud City" (1969), later became part of the partially autobiographical "The Body." Both "Stud City" and its frame again veer from King's trademark horror, embracing the purposes and structures of mainstream fiction and illustrating King's interest in and involvement with such forms.

While at UMO, King also published several poems, again illustrating his exploration of alternative forms and genres. One, "The Dark Man" (Ubris 1969), has proven difficult to locate; without a copy, I can only speculate as to what it was like. However, given the title, King's comments about the influence of Browning's "Childe

Roland to the Dark Tower Came" in the "Afterword"
to The Dark Tower, and the presence of "dark"
characters in works as diverse as The Stand, DT,
and The Talisman, a poem by that title would seem
appropriate for King.

Two other poems, however, are available and
therefore provide more definitive information. In
1971, the year after graduating from UMO, King
published a story, "The Blue Air Compressor," in
Onan, a student literary magazine at UMO. The
story, reprinted with only superficial alterations
in Heavy Metal ten years later (SW 25-28), resembles Poe's "The Tell-tale Heart," to which King
refers several times in the text; to that extent,
it illustrates his increasing skill in his chosen
genre. But the same issue of Onan also contains
an untitled poem by King. Beginning with an image
of "depthless" water in the "key-chords of dawn,"
the poem uses fishing as a metaphor for responsibility. The first stanza emphasizes freedom
through the images of flashing fish and running
water; the second suggests the incremental approach of adult awareness ("love/ is responsibility"), fully developed in the last stanza, in
which fishing becomes responsibility and thus is
put away. The stanzas are unexceptional in structure and development; the metaphors are simultaneously bland and at times confusing, as when
fishing (itself used metaphorically) suddenly
becomes a "loom of complexity," introducing an
uncomfortable Melvillean weaving image. In general, the poem fits nicely into a student literary
magazine. It is competent and mildly interesting
but lacks depth. And it is without any suggestion
of supernatural horror.

Three years earlier, however, King had published another poem. The Fall 1968 issue of Ubris
included a two-page experimental poem, "Harrison
State Park '68" (25-26). Unlike the later poem,
this one exhibits many characteristics associated
with King, beginning with two short quotations
introducing his subject (mental disorders) and
tone ("And I feel like homemade shit."). Where
the later poem is smooth and gently conventional,
this one is rough, its stanzas scattered over the
page like the reality it attempts to describe, its
content hidden among cliches ("If you can't be an
athlete,/ be an athletic supporter") and images of

21

implicit violence. While skirting the supernatural, the poem embraces the kind of horror that emerges in the revised "Strawberry Spring" or "Cain Rose Up," the horror of madness endemic in contemporary society. Its images concentrate on death and violence: Mickey Rooney as Pretty Boy Floyd; a skeleton in Death Valley; monsters induced by nuclear radiation; worms crawling through white grass at midnight. Throughout, King develops the question "Can you do it?" into the same sort of _leitmotif_ that he creates from "Do you love?" in _SC_--and to much the same effect. Love links with death; in the final stanza, the speaker reaches for a hand, only to touch the "radiating five pencils/ of your bones" (26). The poem is by far the more interesting, if only because King speaks here with a more authentic voice.

Perhaps more than anything else, however, King´s writing for The Maine Campus helped him refine his talents. "King´s Garbage Truck," a weekly column running from January 20, 1969 through May 21, 1970, included discussions of student apathy, anti-War protests, and campus politics, as well as reviews of books and films. The columns are fascinating indicators of King´s development, of his wide interests and rapidly developing power as a writer. Some of the columns sound trite and hackneyed; his condemnation of adult perspectives on youth (February 12, 1970) could have been written by almost any young person about to graduate from college in 1969 or 1970. Others are strikingly original, as in his meditation on the frightening power of snow (March 10, 1970), an early non-fictional sketch of ideas later developed in works such as The Shining (1977), "One for the Road" (1977), and--most importantly, almost archetypally--"The Reach" (1981; _SC_ 1985).

In a number of instances, King´s discussion of non-horror materials provided him with seminal images that later became horror stories or novels. In the first column, he reviews the Goddard College dance troupe, specifically a number called "Child of Our Darkness," in which Wynd Winston "portrays a child-woman torn between the forces of light and darkness." The conclusion of the dance, "with burning flames projected onto her body and a

22

screen behind her, was almost numbing in impact,"
and strongly suggests the central image of Firestarter.

Similarly, a column on "strange things in the
world" (December 18, 1969) foreshadows several
later stories. In addition to discussing Judge
Crater, who figures prominently in "The Reaper´s
Image," the column mentions a place called "Jere-
miah´s Lot," a Shaker settlement in Vermont from
which all ihnabitants mysteriously disappeared in
the early 1800s--a clear parallel to ´Salem´s Lot,
"Jerusalem´s Lot," and "One for the Road." The
possibility of a hole punched through our universe
and into another finds fictional expression later
in the DT stories and in "Crouch End" (1980) and
"The Mist" (1980; SC 1985). King´s dream, also
recounted in this column, of a "hideous man with a
scarred face hanging from a black gibbet against a
green sky" immediately suggests scenes from the DT
stories.

"King´s Garbage Truck" ties in directly with
several other works as well: "Cain Rose Up,"
"Strawberry Spring," "Children of the Corn," "The
Cat from Hell," "Uncle Otto´s Truck," "The Fifth
Quarter," "Nona," "The Ballad of the Flexible Bullet," Rage, The Long Walk, Roadwork, The Running
Man (King has a good deal to say about television,
networks, and programming in the "Garbage Truck"),
The Stand, Pet Sematary, and The Talisman. In
each instance, the columns contain passages, often
just a phrase or two, that suggests important
themes or images in King´s later fiction.

The columns deserve a full study themselves
(there will be a chapter on "King´s Garbage Truck"
in The Stephen King Phenomenon), but here it is
sufficient to indicate how extensively they served
as sounding boards for King´s ideas and opinions.
Occasionally they offer unusual insight into his
development as an individual and as a writer. At
least one column seems to contradict an important
point in King´s official biography. Several
studies--including DM (15-28) and Winter´s Art of
Darkness (xv)--refer to King´s first awareness of
threat in the "real" world when the Soviet Union
successfully orbited the first space satellite in
October, 1957. King was ten years old and, "as
was only fitting," at a movie. Even more fitting,
the film was Earth vs. the Flying Saucers. During

the showing, the film stopped and the manager announced that the Russians had "put a space satellite into orbit around the earth. They call it . . . Spootnik" (DM 21).

The reaction was deep silence . . . and fear.

Eleven years earlier, however, in the "Garbage Truck" for May 7, 1970, King looked to graduation by writing about "Where We Are At" and "Where We Were." He recalls important scenes from childhood: a favorite movie (Randolph Scott's Gung Ho), the 1956 Hungarian Revolt and the intense pride it engendered, and Sputnik:

> I was waiting in the barbershop to get a haircut when that happened. I thought it had to be a joke. Americans were always first--we have been with the telephone, the electric light, the airplane--surely the Russians, who played dirty, could not have beaten us into space! It was downright degrading, it was frightening . . . well, it was downright embarrassing.

The reactions are the same, but the scenes differ markedly. King has transformed life into art; the setting in DM is far more powerful as an image than that in the "Garbage Truck" column.

In Christine, Dennis Guilder analyzes fear:

> I had never been so frightened in my life as I was right then. Time passes: the mind rebuilds its defenses. I think one of the reasons there is so little convincing evidence of psychic phenomena is that the mind goes to work and restructures the evidence. A little stacking is better than a lot of insanity. (422)

The issue in question is neither sanity nor psychic phenomena; but it seems possible that King was aware of the intrinsic value of the theater as setting: a small boy, a dark theater, a frightening movie, and the sudden voice announcing doom. The "Garbage Truck" passage relies upon content for effect; the later passage, the result of a decade-long involvement with fiction and writing,

24

adds setting and atmosphere to content, communicating the small boy's fear literally and symbolically. The difference between the two episodes parallels King's own development as a writer.

By the time King graduated from college, then, he had explored several genres. If one adds other tales published before Carrie in 1974, the extent of King's "search for a form" becomes evident. To his science fiction, horror fantasy, and mainstream fiction (including several novels in manuscript), one can add the satire/parody western "Slade," published in weekly installments in The Maine Campus during the summer of 1970 and the "hard-bitten" crime fiction of "The Fifth Quarter" (1972), King's first pseudonymous publication.
Nor is that the end of his explorations. The Talisman (1984) represented a new departure into collaborative fiction as well as into epic-quest and high fantasy. Cycle of the Werewolf began as a calendar; The Eyes of the Dragon is basically a children's story (albeit a remarkably sophisticated one). And King continues to range beyond the limits of horror. For some time, he said recently,

> I've wanted to write a magic carpet
> story. It would be a fantastic story,
> but so far I can't hook it up. It's like
> a car with a bad transmission. . . .
> Actually, I'd like to write an
> Elvis novel. I'd really like to write a
> rock 'n' roll novel. But it's very,
> very hard to write about music, so I
> haven't been able to hook that one up.
> (Modderno)

These are but a few of the many facets of Stephen King; still, they suffice as an introduction to King and to his fiction.
In a larger sense, however, form is secondary to content in Stephen King's writing, a fact that determines the shape of his novels and stories. The narrative itself stands in first position of importance, as opposed to theme or symbol. He is in fact wary of such overtly literary considerations; when they do occur, he says,

I tend to suppress them, because I think conscious structure spoils story. Some editor once described Thomas Wolfe not as a real writer but as 'a divine wind-chime' --that is, an essentially idiotic device through which a breeze or wind might blow, creating pleasant sounds. As Cyndy Lauper says about the Goonies, that's good enough for me. (Letter, 3 August 1985).

Through his explorations of possibilities--early and late--King has enabled himself to represent the real and the unreal, the rational and the ir-rational, in ways that highlight the implicit power of his narratives. He is comfortable in mainstream and horror, in psychological suspense and science fiction. And through all, his concern for the underlying story shows through, thrilling, chilling, and entertaining his readers.

Chapter III

ALONG THE MAIN STREAM:

Rage, The Long Walk, Sword in the Darkness,
Blaze, and Roadwork

When Frank Belknap Long was asked by Twilight
Zone Magazine to assess contemporary horror-
writers, he mentioned Stephen King specifically:

> Many present-day writers have greater
> maturity, greater insight than the hor-
> ror writers of the 1920s or 1930s. I
> think every powerful new writer who has
> come along has contributed something new
> and important. Stephen King, for exam-
> ple, has taken ordinary situations, sit-
> uations that confront young people in,
> let us say, the average American vil-
> lage, and has dwelt in a totally
> naturalistic way on how they act and
> react. He has made all of this so real-
> istic that when he introduces an element
> of supernatural horror, you wholly be-
> lieve it. (Collins 18)

Long pinpoints perhaps the most effective stylistic technique in King's fiction--the inexorable
sense of reality subtly transforming into real-
ity-gone-wrong. The characteristic is present in
all of King's horror fiction, not a particularly
surprising discovery in light of King's long apprenticeship in writing "realistic" fiction.
    Until 1977, all of his published novels were
to some degree horror fiction; in 1977, he published his first non-horror novel, Rage, but only
under the Bachman pseudonym. Not until Different
Seasons (1982) did he publish non-horror fiction
under his own name. Even before Carrie appeared
in 1974, however, King had written several novels,
few of them overtly supernatural horror. Because
he needed to preserve the integrity of the Bachman

27

pseudonym, lists of those early manuscript novels
have frequently been vague as to number and order
of composition; in a letter sent in August 1985,
however, King clarified the matter considerably by
providing the following information:

* Getting It On, begun in the summer of 1966,
  completed and submitted in late 1971 or early
  1972, and finally published as Rage (1977),
  the first "Bachman novel";

* The Long Walk (1979), published as the second
  "Bachman" novel but written during 1966-
  1967, King's freshman year at UMO--his first
  finished novel;

* Sword in the Darkness, which Winter calls
  King's second novel (Art xvi-xvii); King also
  referred to this manuscript as Babylon Here
  when discussing his early manuscripts because, as he says, "I wanted to throw sand in
  the eyes of people who might think I was
  Bachman";

* Blaze, written around 1970, a "reworking of
  Steinbeck's Of Mice and Men and kind of a
  ghost story." In spite of King's comments in
  the "Afterword" to DS, this was not the manuscript submitted to Bill Thompson along with
  Second Coming ('Salem's Lot);

* The Running Man (1982), the fourth "Bachman"
  novel, written during a weekend in 1971,
  shortly after King completed the first draft
  for Carrie. His initial impulse was that The
  Running Man was much stronger than Carrie,
  but submissions to Doubleday and DAW resulted
  in rejection slips;

* Roadwork (1981), the third "Bachman" novel,
  written in 1974 "in roughly the time-frame of
  the novel itself," just after King completed
  'Salem's Lot. (Letter, 3 August 1985)

In addition, the bibliography in Fear Itself refers to a final manuscript, The Cannibals as "a
novel, publication plans indefinite" (268). While
no date is mentioned, the title appears among the

pre-_Carrie_ works.

Most of the manuscripts share a single characteristic: they seem as much mainstream as supernatural horror. The Running Man and The Long Walk
are minimally science-fictional and thus could be
considered non-mainstream; King mentions Blaze as
"kind of" a ghost story, the only overt mention of
the supernatural in the listing. As important as
it is to establish the chronology of composition
for those early works, it is equally important to
note the kind of novels King considered as he
began his career. The fact that King completed at
least eight novels before seeing Carrie in print
in 1974 demonstrates his dedication to writing,
while the parallel fact that of the eight half are
predominantly mainstream illustrates the depth of
King's apprenticeship in writing novels outside
the narrow limits of supernatural horror. From
this apprenticeship arises the incessant sense
throughout his writing that his worlds are real,
his characters believable, and his narratives both
plausible and possible, regardless of how incredible developments may become.

The earliest extended manifestation of King's
mastery over what C. S. Lewis called "realism of
presentation" occurs in manuscripts such as Rage
or The Long Walk, novels that owe as much to traditional, mainstream literature as to supernatural
horror. As important as horror has been in King's
career, it has never been exclusive. As early as
the "Garbage Truck" columns, for instance, King
showed a remarkable diversity of interests. Only
twice did he devote columns entirely to horror:
once to a review of novels, including Robert
Bloch's The Dead Beat, Richard Matheson's The
Shrinking Man, Michael Avallone's The Coffin
Things, and Bram Stoker's Dracula (27 June 1969);
and once to a discussion of a series of films
sponsored by the UMO Memorial Union Activities
Board, including Rosemary's Baby, Psycho, Dracula,
Frankenstein, and The Pit and the Pendulum (19
February 1970).

Otherwise, the columns cover a wide range of
topics: films as divergent as Easy Rider and If
It's Tuesday, This Must Be Belgium; contemporary
poetry, especially the works of Howard Nemerov,
Richard Wilbur, Constance Hunting, and Ron Loewen-
sohn; birth control; the California grape boycott;

the moon walk; television, the generation gap; and
trivia quizzes. Although many columns suggest
images or themes that later appear in King's horror novels and stories, even more concern themselves with analyzing King's world--the people,
places, and events that mattered to him and to his
fellow students.

This concern finds its way into King's earliest manuscripts.

After the publication of Stephen King as
Richard Bachman, it seems repetitive to discuss
the Bachman novels. It is worthwhile, however, in
order to gain a necessary perspective on King's
subsequent fictions. In addition, the novels are
worth more attention than they have received, both
as King's first attempts at novels and as completed works in their own right.

Rage, for example, is not only among King's
earliest full-length manuscripts, but it is also a
highly detailed, highly convincing examination of
the pressures and frustrations endemic to American
school systems. Charlie Decker's responses to
situations are admittedly extreme: shooting two
teachers, threatening several others, holding a
class hostage, and forcing administrators and
police officials to confront their own levels of
fear and frustration. Yet in another sense, the
novel is not that extreme; it defines the shifting, tenuous relationships in most contemporary
high schools and, to a lesser extent, colleges.
It translates those relationships into explosive,
often heavily sexual actions, but beneath the fic-
tive elements the reader can discern seeds of
truth, which King also examined in several "Garbage Truck" columns.

> Want me to tell you a bad thing?
> Okay. I will. It's a bad thing to wake
> up in the middle of the night, light a
> cigarette, and wonder what the hell you
> are doing in this place. That's pretty
> bad. But it's worse if you don't have
> any kind of answer. ("GT" 8 May 1969)

Although this passage is part of King's
non-fiction discussion of student pressures for
The Maine Campus, it could have appeared in any of
several places in Rage. Charlie Decker's funda-

30

mental questions are the same; the answers he posits are also King's. The column continues, drawing pessimistic thumbnail sketches of faculty members "painted into an academic corner with no place to stretch and no room to breathe"; of students crushed beneath "requirements, irrelevant courses, and a suffocating feeling of futility," with the survivors facing futures of interminable soap operas, stultifying careers, and heart-attacks at thirty-five (a motif that recurs in Thinner, with even more personal meaning for King, who had by then entered heart-attack country). For the students in Rage, for Barton George Dawes in Roadwork, for William Halleck in Thinner, life is a "shaky cease-fire" (RW).

That these concerns should first appear in Rage is understandable. Half of it was written during the summer of 1966, between King's graduation from high school and his entrance into college, and completed in the summer of 1971, while King was working at the New Franklin Laundry in Bangor. As a result, it is adolescent in tone and content, in theme and vitality. It reflects King's fears and frustrations, not only as a student, but as an adult. School is "a pressure cooker, sure," he writes in the "Garbage Truck" columns:

> We all know that. But the thing that scares me at three in the morning is that I'm afraid the pressure-cooker effect doesn't stop with graduation. Things don't look much better. (8 May 1969).

A year later, his views had become even more pessimistic. In his final column, a mock announcement of his birth "into the real world," he defined his political stance as "Extremely radical, largely due to the fact that nobody seems to listen to you unless you threaten to shut them down, turn them off, or make some kind of trouble." Under "future prospects," he wrote: "Hazy, although either nuclear annihilation or environmental strangulation seem to be definite possibilities" (21 May 1970).

The result of these questions, problems, and fears was a series of novels that reflected King's attitudes. Rage was begun in 1966; even before

31

completing it, however, King wrote three more novels. The Long Walk was written in 1968-1969, while King was a freshman at UMO. The premise came to him while he was hitchhiking home from college one night: a sporting event in a future America, in which one hundred boys would walk until they died, the last one winning the Prize: anything he wanted for the rest of his life. Although science fiction in its future setting, the novel is firmly grounded in realism. Garraty and his fellow walkers follow highways King knew well; they suffer the same insecurities and identity crises that the young King refers to in his "Garbage Truck" columns; and they are victims of the same insensitive if not inimical adult establishment he had already begun describing in Rage. The Long Walk expands King's vision, moving outward from the narrow focus of a high-school classroom to encompass an entire society. The Long Walk effects the America of the future economically, politically, and socially; the Walkers become sacrificial victims expended in order to insure stability and prosperity.

The novel is an unusually strong achievement for a twenty-one-year-old writer. King manages to create empathy as well as sympathy for the pains Garraty and the others endure during the Long Walk. He handles their immaturity and emotional outbursts with restraint, while simultaneously instilling the readers with a sense of psychological horror as the Walk progresses, as children die in agony amid the cheers of the great god Crowd. Its apocalyptic final scene is the culmination of a novel that exhausts its readers, literally and physically as well as symbolically and emotionally.

King's third novel, Sword in the Darkness (which he has also referred to as Babylon Here) again expands the scope of his vision. About a race riot in a city called Harding, it too indicates another facet of King's social consciousness. In early 1970, shortly after finishing the manuscript for Sword in the Darkness, King reviewed George Kennedy's film Tick . . . Tick . . . Tick, concentrating in one paragraph on the film's awareness of the complexities of racial tensions:

> the movie treats some of the prob-
> lems of white-black relations in the
> south with clarity and humanity (what do
> you do when a black man commits rape?
> What do you do when a white 16-year-old
> boy gets liquored up and causes a car
> accident which kills a small girl?)
> . . . .

The film, King notes, fails to consider the
situations fully; "the ultimate result," he concludes, "is just a little too sugary sweet--the
Kleegle of the local KKK ends up Changing His Ways
and helping [Jim] Brown and Kennedy turn back an
avenging posse of vigilantes, which is determined
to free one of Brown's white prisoners" (26
February 1970).

Sword in the Darkness was King's opportunity
to explore the problems and resolutions of racial
tensions for himself. Unfortunately, the novel
did not succeed: "it is a very bad book," he
writes. "I can't even like it when I'm drunk"
(Letter, 3 August 1985).

The fourth novel, Blaze, was written around
1970--essentially, King had worked on four novels
in as many years, while still not yet twenty-three
years old. This novel, he has noted, was based on
Steinbeck's Of Mice and Men, much as The Long Walk
reflected Shirley Jackson's "The Lottery." It was
a "kind of ghost story," the first mention among
King's early manuscript novels of anything overtly
supernatural. And it was unpublishable:

> It wasn't a terrible novel, but ab-
> surdly downbeat and ultimately corny.
> . . . I came close to publishing it as a
> Bachman and pulled it at almost the last
> minute, after a sober reading of the re-
> written manuscript. The goddam thing
> was so dismal it made "The Little Match
> Girl" look like "Pollyanna." (Letter, 3
> August 1985).

Following the completion of Carrie in manuscript, King wrote one final mainstream novel,
Roadwork. Taking place during the "First Energy
Crisis" of late 1973 and early 1974, the novel examines the disintegration of Barton George Dawes

under the multiple pressures of a changing economy, a failing marriage, his increasing alienation from others, and--overshadowing all else--the earlier death of his son from cancer. The novel in fact seems almost as much about cancer as about Dawes: cancer as disease, cancer as metaphor for destructive relationships, cancer as symbol of the unknowable and uncontrollable in human lives. Like Rage and The Long Walk, the novel stems from King's experiences, although in this case a far more critical one: the death of his mother to cancer shortly before. As with "The Woman in the Room" (NS, 1978), life provided the stimulus for a strong work, giving the novel an additional touch of emotional realism that makes reading it an unusually moving experience. The pressures Dawes encounters are not extraordinary; the tragedy of his destruction becomes even more tragic with King's clear suggestion that such things happen in the real world. None of us is immune.

As with Blaze, King was influenced in writing Roadwork. The references to Nick Adams throughout suggests Ernest Hemingway's fictional hero (SK/RB 74-77, 83-85), although King considers Kurt Vonnegut's Slaughterhouse Five as the most direct influence. His use of white space and signs in Roadwork was an attempt at re-creating the resonance of Vonnegut's repeated "So it goes" (Letter, 3 August 1985).

As noted earlier, Roadwork was submitted with Second Coming as a follow-up to Carrie's success. Thompson chose the horror novel, and King embarked on a series of enormously successful novels, all in some degree touched with the supernatural and the horrific. Still, he did not completely divorce himself from mainstream fiction. "The Woman in the Room," is among his finest pieces; the film made from it is equally successful in defining the difficult decisions faced by a man who must watch his mother dying slowly and painfully. "The Last Rung on the Ladder" (NS) is a similarly powerful anatomy of fragile relations and human interdependence. Nor is it coincidental, I think, that both stories appeared first in King's collection, rather than separately in magazines or periodicals. Strong as they are, they are not what readers expected of him.

With Different Seasons, King's abilities to

34

write non-horror fiction came to the fore. Only "The Breathing Method" diverges into the fantastic; the remaining three are stridently and consciously realistic stories of hope, maturity, and despair. Since Different Seasons was discussed at length by David Engebretson in The Shorter Works of Stephen King, little more need be said here except, as with the Bachman novels, to emphasize their importance in King's development. His "brand-name technique" succeeds to the extent that it does because he understands and analyzes his world, then replicates it with uncanny intensity. Events in The Shining, The Stand, or Christine, for example, seem believable because of the context King places them in. Nor is it difficult to see how little a space there is between a story such as "Apt Pupil," which develops horror out of the everyday and the possible (however improbable), and a novel like Cujo, which adds but the slightest suggestion of the supernatural and thus qualifies as a "horror" novel.

By 1974, then, King had come a long way. He had written eight novels, published one, and prepared himself for the most spectacularly successful career in contemporary horror fantasy. But throughout, he retains close connections with mainstream writing and with his own past.

NOTES

[1] In late 1971 or early 1972, King submitted Rage under the title Getting It On, a phrase from a song by T. Rex called "Bang a Gong (Get It On)." Doubleday was interested, but finally rejected it. It was originally submitted under the pseudonym Guy Pillsbury (King's maternal grandfather and "a Jud Crandall prototype if ever there was one" [Letter, 3 August 1985]). Later, when NAL accepted it, the editors noted that the Pillsbury name appeared on contracts with King's. When a phone call came asking him to create a new pseudonym, King was listening to Bachman-Turner Overdrive on the stereo and a novel by Richard Stark lay on his desk--thus, Richard Bachman.

Thinner's dust-jacket photograph, which misled many readers and continues to raise an occasional question about Richard Bachman's identity

in spite of King´s having acknowledged the novels,
is of a friend of King´s agent.

Chapter IV

INTO THE TWILIGHT LANDS:

Carrie, Cujo, The Dead Zone,
Firestarter, and Thinner

Early in Cujo, King describes Red Razberry
Zingers as "somewhere in the twilight zone between
cereal and candy" (30). Not quite either one,
Zingers are difficult to classify, except as a
source of trouble for Vic Trenton.

A parallel cross-classification occurs among
several of King's novels which, like Red Razberry
Zingers, seem to exist in a "twilight zone," not
quite horror, not quite supernatural fantasy, not
quite science fiction (in spite of Joseph Patrouch's arguments), and not quite mainstream. In
Carrie, Cujo and The Dead Zone, King relies only
marginally on the supernatural, despite surface
suggestions that the novels are intended as horror. In all three, he insists upon defining episodes as clearly explainable. With Firestarter,
he moves closer to horror while still maintaining
both a respectable distance and the illusion that
situations are ultimately and objectively explainable. In Thinner, he asserts the supernatural,
blurring the borders between mainstream and horror.

As if to provide transition from the more or
less mainstream fiction of the early Bachman novels into supernatural horror, King wrote several
stories and novels that illustrate his interest in
the "twilight lands" between genres. "Strawberry
Spring," for example, indicates several changes in
King's artistic and literary directions. The
first version, published in Ubris in 1968, concentrates on psychological suspense; the horror in
the story, if any exists, stems from King's highly
effective descriptions, from the sense of an un-

37

known lurking in the warm fogs of an unseasonal
spring. The revision, published a decade later in
Night Shift with intermediate appearances in Cavalier and Gent, shows a Stephen King more aware of
the potential of horror and turning that potential
back on the reader. After impelling empathy with
the unnamed first-person narrator (an unusual narrative stance for King), King reverses positions
by revealing that the narrator not only fears the
killer but is the killer. Fear and terror infuse
the story, but there is nothing specifically supernatural.

With Carrie (1974), the situation becomes
more complicated. As his first book, it set the
directions which subsequent novels would follow
and which forced King to publish his non-horror
novels under the Bachman pseudonym. From the beginning, King´s career as a novelist has been
marked by an emphasis on the horrific. The dust
jacket for the hardcover edition of Carrie represents typical attitudes toward King:

> . . . **Stephen King** reveals a New England
> town, a girl, and a secret older than
> history. His chilling tale takes hold
> of the reader, from the first bizarre
> incident to the last blossoming terror.

Overstated (as dust-jacket blurbs frequently are),
the appraisal at least partially misleads readers.
The "secret older than history" must be telekinesis, but if so, the statement becomes doubly problematical.

If telekinesis is indeed "older than history," it can only with difficulty be defined as
"supernatural," and the results of Carrie White´s
explosive telekinesis become horror only in a limited sense; that is, the experiences and descriptions may be graphic and bloody, but they do not
stir the deepest levels of fear . . . fear of the
unknown and the unknowable.

In addition, King himself takes pains in the
text to raise telekinesis from the level of myth
and legend and place it on a marginally scientific
footing. The opening pages of the novel urge the
reader to view Carrie´s paranormal ability in
calm, rational terms: "Nobody was really sur-
prised when it happened," King asserts, only then

hinting at the horrific: "not at the subconscious level where savage things grow." The girls who abuse Carrie are "shocked, thrilled, ashamed, or simply glad" at the effects of their hazing but not horrified or terrified. Their claims to surprise are "of course" untrue:

> Carrie had been going to school with some of them since the first grade, and this had been building since all that time, building slowly and immutably, in accordance with all the laws that govern human nature, building with all the steadiness of a chain reaction approaching critical mass.
> What none of them knew, of course, was that Carrie White was telekinetic. (3-4)

The tone and diction are all carefully neutral; with few exceptions, King does not yet telegraph horror through word choice, as is the case with many other writers and in many other novels. Instead, he creates a feeling of calmness, of objectivity, stipulating that Carrie´s actions and reactions are natural and inevitable. Carrie´s world is, as the text says, a twilight land of paradoxical probabilities, "a real world where nightmares happen" (24).

Certainly his approach in Carrie differs from that of more traditional "horror" novels. From the first paragraph, for example, T.E.D. Klein´s The Ceremonies leaves no doubt about its nature:

> The city lies throbbing in the sunlight. From its heart a thin black thread of smoke coils lazily toward the sky. April is almost thirteen hours dead: already the world has changed. (9)

"Throbbing," "black," "coils," "dead," "change"-- the diction defines the thrust of the novel.

Even more explicitly, Frank de Felitta´s Golgotha Falls uses the opening pages to define both the genre and the reader´s expectations:

> Golgotha Falls, 1890, north Massachusetts. The town lay in a hollow of

> hard, obdurate terrain where the stag-
> nant ponds bred crawling mites on
> browned, drooping reeds. Siloam Creek
> choked on detritus from the woolen mills
> and there, on the clay bank, the Catho-
> lic merchants from the nearby town of
> Lawrence decided to build their church.
>   The ground when broken was sandy.
> Indians, long dead and disinterred from
> the loose soil, had to be carted away in
> skeletal heaps. (7)

Within two more paragraphs, de Felitta conjures a
"stench like sour milk" emanating from "fissured"
bedrock, cracked timbers that kill four workmen,
diphtheria, malaria, and seven new graves behind
an iron gate . . . a substantially different atmosphere from Carrie.
    King is, of course, capable of asserting the
horrific within the first few words of a story or
novel. The imagistic echoes of Poe and Lovecraft
in the openings of "The Glass Floor" (1967) or
"The Blue Air Compressor" (1971, 1981), or the
gray skies and rotting pumpkins of "It Grows on
You" (1975) define King's intentions in those
stories; among his novels, Thinner is perhaps the
best example of a clear-cut introduction into the
world of horror. It is, as Kirby McCauley noted,
more like a King book than a Bachman, and several
reviewers argued explicitly that no one but King
could have written the first paragraph:

>   "Thinner," the old Gypsy man with
> the rotting nose whispers to William Hal-
> leck. . . . "Thinner." And before Halleck
> can jerk away, the old Gypsy reaches out
> and caresses his cheek with one twisted
> finger. His lips spread open like a
> wound, showing a few tombstone stumps
> poking out of his gums. They are black
> and green. His tongue squirms between
> them and then slides out to slick his
> grinning, bitter lips. (1)

Set against such imagery, Carrie seems sedate
and controlled. King's initial quotation from the
"Westover (Me.) weekly Enterprise, August 19,
1966," enhances the realistic tone, implying that

40

what follows must be truthful and accurate; any
doubters can simply check the apropriate issue of
the newspaper. The neutral, objective, and precise
diction of the article itself reinforces the tone.
Horror becomes more image than action, more simile
than reality. Carrie sees ivy cloaking the White
bungalow "_like_ a grotesque giant hand ridged with
great veins which had sprung up out of the ground
to grip the building" (21; my italics), an image
that asserts an external horror more in keeping
with de Palma's film than King's fiction. Similarly, when Estelle Horan speaks of Carrie, her
expression changes to make her look "more _like_
Lovecraft out of Arkham than Kerouac out of South-
ern California" (22; my italics)--again the emphasis on a simile asserting but not demonstrating
horror.

In this respect, _Carrie_ parallels other recent novels that blend the subjectivity of fantasy
and horror with the objectivity of science fiction
by providing scientific (or pseudoscientific) explanations for monsters, creatures, or other paraphernalia of horror:

* Colin Wilson's _The Mind Parasites_ (1967) and
  The Space Vampires (1976), the latter describing aliens discovered in a derelict ship
  in terms drawn from traditional vampire motifs, then re-defining the aliens as fugitive
  entities from another galaxy;

* Peter Straub's _If You Could See Me Now_ (1977)
  and _Ghost Story_ (1979), which explain ghosts
  as objectively observable shape-shifters
  co-existent with humanity;

* Whitley Strieber's _The Wolfen_ (1978), _The
  Hunger_ (1980), _Black Magic_ (1981), and _The
  Night Church_ (1983), each re-defining traditional horror figures--werewolves, vampires,
  demons--in contemporary scientific terms;

* F. Paul Wilson's _The Keep_ (1981), which sub-
  verts the entire panoply of vampire mythology
  by revealing that the supposed vampire belongs to a species pre-dating humanity;

* Dean Koontz' _Phantasms_ (1983), which connects

41

Koontz's amorphous monster with mysterious disappearances throughout history.

In each instance, the writers consciously subvert the fantastic by shifting to logical, rational (or rational-seeming) explanations for phenomena an earlier generation of novelists might have asserted simply as supernatural (Collings, "Filling the Niche"). In <u>Carrie</u>, as in <u>The Dead Zone</u>, <u>Cujo</u>, and <u>Firestarter</u>, King applies a similar technique.

King's ambivalence toward genre characterizes <u>Carrie</u>, particularly in its dual narrative structure. Although much of the non-narrative material was added in later drafts to bring the novel up to a minimum length (Winter 196; Warren 17), the interpolations seem critical to the tone of the novel. Ben P. Indick writes that fear is so important to King's next two novels ('Salem's Lot and <u>The Shining</u>) that "in retrospect it is surprising how small a part it plays in <u>Carrie</u> . . ." (9-10). If one of King's purposes is to touch wellsprings of fear within his readers, as he has argued in <u>Danse Macabre</u>, <u>Carrie</u> seems almost counterproductive. Instead of creating an escalating narrative beginning and ending in blood and terror (as in de Palma's film version), King interrupts the narrative with excerpts from "documentary" studies written <u>after</u> the cataclysm that destroys Chamberlain, Maine. The interpolations simultaneously reassure the reader that ultimately all will be resolved (someone must, like Melville's Ishmael, be able to say "And I only am escaped alone to tell thee") and create suspense . . . but not horror. We are told, for example, that a character has only two hours to live; such structures are invariably neutrally worded, avoiding any implicit evocations of horror. They startle and shock, but do not inspire horror.

In addition, King emphasizes the objectivity of the interpolations. Quotations appear from <u>The Shadow Exploded: Documented Facts and Specific Conclusions Derived from the Case of Carietta White</u>, ostensibly published by Tulane University Press. Key words in the title--"documented facts," "conclusions," "derived," "case"--enhance the illusion of reality, as does King's crediting the book to a university press, which would tend toward academic conservatism rather than sensation-

alism. The horror might have been far more explicit had King quoted from Richard Dees' Inside
Views, as he would do later in The Dead Zone.

Equally convincing (if something of an inside
joke) is the brief reference to Carrie's sev-
enth-grade poetry (57). The passage furthers the
reader's empathy for Carrie, particularly as it
quotes verbatim from her teacher, Edwin King.
Coming from the pen of Stephen Edwin King, teacher
of English at Hampden Academy, publishing poet,
and empathetic human being, the passage ties the
novel closer to the twilight land, that "real
world where nightmares happen."

Any potential sensationalism, as in references to Susan Snell's My Name is Susan Snell or
Jack Gasver's Carrie: The Black Dawn (appearing in
the September 12, 1980 issue of a popular magazine, Esquire), is countered by other outside
"sources": Ogilvie's Dictionary of Psychic Phenomena; Dean D. L. McGuffin's "Telekinesis: Analysis
and Aftermath" (Science Yearbook 1981); Black
Prom: The White Commission Report, sponsored by
the State Investigatory Board of Maine and published by Signet in 1980 (another inside joke;
Carrie was published in paperback by Signet, as
were all of King's paperback reprints); and the
New England and national AP tickers.

The brief "Part Three: Wreckage" accentuates
the sense of documentary realism, as King includes
the "Westover Mercy Hospital/Report of Decease"
for Carrie White and further references from The
Shadow Exploded and My Name is Susan Snell. By the
end of the novel, Carrie's experiences have become
so integrated into "reality" that King includes an
entry from John R. Coombs' Slang Terms Explained
defining "to rip off a Carrie" (198), implying
that the events in Chamberlain have passed beyond
sensationalism to become part of normal human
activities.

The final interpolation, from Amelia Jenks'
letter of 1988, confirms what King has suggested
from the beginning: Carrie White's outburst of
telekinetic destruction is not something supernatural. It has happened before; it will surely, in-
evitably happen again.

The joke, of course, is that all of King's
excerpts are as fictional as the narratives inter-
woven with them. Like the scientific references

43

in The Dead Zone and Firestarter, however, they create the illusion of reality. Indeed, King even provides a marginally scientific explanation for Carrie White. She is the victim of a "genetic-regressive occurrence," similar to but opposite from hemophilia (81-82). The condition manifests only in women, and then under specified physiological and psychological conditions (100). Regardless of how unconvincing the explanation may be, King does not simply assert horror as he does in 'Salem's Lot, Christine, Thinner, The Talisman or Cycle of the Werewolf. To that extent, Carrie is almost as much science fiction as horror.

Much more could and should be said about Carrie (and will be in The Films of Stephen King). Carrie depends on heavily symbolic overtones, as has been noted in Chelsea Quinn Yarbro's discussion of its mythic and fairy-tale motifs. Douglas Winter effectively anatomizes characterization, King's underlying romanticism, and Carrie as a vehicle for discussing the dangers implicit in growing up--a recurring theme in King's fiction.

For this study, however, it is sufficient to suggest that in spite of popular and critical attitudes toward King as the modern master of horror, there is more to Carrie than that. It neatly balances divergent perspectives; it carefully interweaves the visceral and the rational, the subjective and the objective, the horrific and the scientific. Even its radically differing prose textures blend to create a work that transcends easy classification.

Many of the techniques King used in Carrie recur in Cujo (1981). The later novel exhibits the same ambivalence of treatment and atmosphere, with the difference that in Cujo, King moves even further from the supernatural to concentrate on events that could in fact happen. In spite of the Sharp Cereal Professor's repeated assurance, "Nope, nothing wrong here," there is decidedly something wrong in the Castle Rock of Cujo. Each character understands that. Vic Trenton confronts the dissolution of his business; Donna Trenton, the prospect of a disintegrating marriage. Tad Trenton faces the symbolic monster in the closet; Brett Camber, the monster-father in the barn. Joe Camber tries to understand a world beyond his com-

44

prehension and retreats into drunkenness and boorishness; Charity Camber watches her son gradually
falling into the same traits and traps. Steve
Kemp turns back to a wasted past; Gary Pervier
watches an empty future stretch interminably before him.

Castle Rock and its inhabitants still struggle under the shadow of Frank Dodd, dead six years
yet present in their memories and imaginations.
Although King may have added the Dodd references
in a later draft (Winter, _Art_ 97), they work
structurally to unite _Cujo_. The evil is external,
not simply a result of Donna Trenton's infidelity,
Joe Camber's boorishness, or Gary Pervier's drunk-
en cynicism. It seems, for example, as if King
disposes of George Bannermann crudely and harshly
in _Cujo_. A single lapse in following police pro-
cedures results in Bannerman's violent and horrib-
ly painful death. In other ways, however, that
death _is_ appropriate. In his last moments, Bannerman sees (or thinks he sees) the spectre of
Frank Dodd in Cujo's eyes (285). It is as if he
finally confronts the truth he missed with such
devastating results in _The Dead Zone_; his death
approaches an atonement.

This unrelenting feeling of things gone desperately wrong makes _Cujo_ painfully difficult to
read . . . and even more difficult to _re_-read. In
spite of the publicity hype for _Pet Sematary_ as
the "story so horrifying he was unsure of when it
should be published" or the novel that makes it
"possible for Stephen King to terrify even himself" (Doubleday), _Cujo_ seems more threatening on
a second reading. One can dismiss _Pet Sematary_;
after having once followed the trajectory of fear
and death, re-reading the novel is an intellectual
exercise, a stretching of imagination rather than
an exploration into visceral terror. One can,
after all, simply relegate the Wendigo and the
horror it brings to handy mental boxes: myth, legend, fantasy of the darker kind. And, of course,
no one _really_ comes back from the dead like Church
or Gage.

Cujo is far more difficult to dismiss, either
as novel or as film, because it is _not_ an exercise
in the imagination. Unlike _'Salem's Lot_ or _Chris-
tine_ or _Cycle of the Werewolf_, _Cujo_ could occur
without any substantive alterations in our percep-

45

tion of the universe. The evil in Cujo may simply
be reality itself--a harsh world where otherwise
good men develop mental and sexual aberrations
that transform them into vicious killers, or where
otherwise good dogs (and King says repeatedly that
Cujo was one of those rare good dogs) develop
rabies and kill.

To that extent, the "monster in the closet"
becomes more metaphorical than horrific. In spite
of its emphatic fairy-tale beginning, with the
phrase "Once upon a time" isolated on the first
page, or its frequent references to situations as
being like fairy tales, Cujo is stridently realistic. The opening paragraphs define the monster
that had afflicted Castle Rock:

> He was not werewolf, vampire, ghoul,
> or unnameable creature from the enchanted
> forest or from the snowy wastes; he was
> only a cop named Frank Dodd with mental
> and sexual problems. (2)

Frank Dodd kills himself in The Dead Zone; the
physical manifestation of the "monster" disappears. But as King notes, the monster can never
die: "It came to Castle Rock again in the summer
of 1980" (3). Even more critically, King suggests
that the monster has been present all along in
sublimated forms, long before the minor outbreak
of rabies that results in four deaths. Brett Camber began sleepwalking and having bad dreams in
1974, when he was only four years old (the same
age as Tad at the time of the novel). George Bannermann has not forgotten Frank Dodd, nor has the
rest of Castle Rock. Mothers and grandmothers
frighten children into obedience by conjuring his
name and image, keeping alive the essence of the
monster.

Thus, to a large extent, Tad´s monster in the
closet seems as much a metaphor as manifestation
--a suggestion King develops throughout. Again
and again, he presents images of false horror:
toilet bowls full of blood are really only the
result of a chemical dye; Charity Camber has a
premonition of her son´s death in the barn, a pre-
sentiment undeveloped in the novel; the back of
the Trenton´s Pinto looks as if someone had committed hari-kiri there (an intriguing foreshadow-

46

ing, implying that Tad´s death is both ritual and sacrificial), but it is only spilled ketchup. Elsewhere, King creates the texture of horror by judiciously placing emphatic adjectives in otherwise innocuous sentences. Vic refers to his discovery of Donna´s infidelity as "grisly dessert following a putrid main course" (91-92); only the critical words "grisly" and "putrid" transform the passage into horror. Cujo is "<u>like</u> a horror-movie monster" (156); Donna´s sudden fear that the Cambers are lying dead in the barn strikes her as "gargoyle-<u>like</u>" (180; my italics). The structural <u>like</u> turns reality into simile, denying the sense of the supernatural. Similarly vampires appear . . . in a dream; Vic enters the Narnia-like horror landscape of the closet . . . but only in his dream (185-186).

Still, King does allow characters to confront the monster. Tad sees it in the closet; Donna recognizes a malevolent sentience in the mad dog´s eyes; Vic Trenton hears his son´s voice from the closet, and George Bannerman recognizes Frank Dodd in Cujo´s eyes. Yet in each instance, the characters are under inordinate stress--Bannerman stands within moments of death--and their perceptions, like perceptions throughout the novel, are distorted. They might be seeing tricks of light and shadow, as in Tad´s case, or hallucinating.

On the other hand, King explicitly highlights the impossibly coincidental events that isolate Donna and Tad on Camber´s farm: a faulty dye-lot, a stuck pin in a carburetor, Charity Camber winning something for the first (and as even she realizes, the <u>only</u>) time in her life and standing up to her husband; Vic´s isolation from Donna because of the Sharps debacle and her infidelity; Steve Kemp´s decision to trash the Trenton home, throwing both Vic and the police momentarily off track; Camber´s stopping his mail delivery; Bannerman´s decision (out of character, given what we know of him from <u>The Dead Zone</u>) to break procedure when he sees the battered Pinto in the Camber´s yard. All of these situations, focusing as they do on Tad Trenton dying in the sun, suggest a larger force at work than mere coincidence.

There is, of course, a reason for the seemingly inevitable progression of events. As King´s mock hero Slade says, he rescues Sandra Dawson in the nick of time because he always does--"Steve King sees to that" (<u>Maine Campus</u> 23 July 1970). The deadly sequence leading to Tad's death occurs because Stephen King so orders his fictional universe. Yet in this case, even King was caught by surprise. In a question session at the Conference on the Fantastic in the Arts (March 1984), King was asked why he let Tad die. His response was that he had not intended to; from the beginning, Tad was to live, as in King's original screenplay, the basis for Don Carlos Dunaway and Lauren Currier's final version. Instead, King said, he had Donna push Vic away from Tad's body and begin giving the boy artificial respiration; only when he realized that twenty minutes had passed (306) did King accept Tad's death as irrevocable, an explanation for the repeated "Tad was still dead" threading through the final pages of the novel.

In this world--and in the world of <u>Cujo</u>--dogs do develop rabies and little boys do die. it isn't pleasant; it just is.

The feeling that Cujo is a monster or even (as Jean Strouse argues) possessed by the evil spirit of Frank Dodd is at best ambivalent. For every passage linking Cujo with Dodd or suggesting that events lie outside the natural order of things, King provides an equal and opposite passage, culminating in the final paragraphs of the novel. The characters have departed. The Trentons are resuming their shattered lives and, finally, for them "it was a little better. A little" (316). The Cambers have a new dog and a new life, one far more hope-filled than the old one. And Cujo is gone. Divorced from the emotional weight of events, the narrative voice speaks calmly and soothingly:

> It would perhaps not be amiss to point out that he had always tried to be a good dog. . . . He had never wanted to kill anybody. He had been struck by something, possibly destiny, or fate, or only a degenerative nerve disease called rabies. Free will was not a factor. (318)

If there is a "monster" in <u>Cujo</u>, it is life itself . . . or perhaps <u>time</u>, since with one exception, the major characters in the novel are obsessed by age and the passing of time. Aunt Evie, like Stella Flanders of "The Reach" the oldest member of her community and a harbinger of change, is fully absorbed by time--her status is a result of her having experienced more of it than anyone else. Tad Trenton, on the other end, is almost unaware of time and the changes it brings. Only with difficulty can he recognize an older version of himself in his dream (another false foreshadowing, since he will not live that long). For him, life is present-tense. Between these two lies a range of characters effected (and afflicted) by time. Donna's fears of aging impel her into the abortive affair with Kemp; his vanity, coupled by the discovery of gray hair in his beard, stimulates his violent response to her rejection. Charity Camber sees how time had worn her and her sister; even more critically, she sees Brett adopting his father's worst characteristics. Gary Pervier lives in a lost past, uncaring of any future at all. He almost lives to die, and finally gets his wish. Bannerman's past is haunted by his disastrous failure to connect Frank Dodd with the series of murders--this connection with <u>The Dead Zone</u> gives Bannerman's death an air of penance and restitution as he equates the mad dog with an earlier incident of madness.

It is as if King intends Tad as a sacrifice. The one character untouched by time dies. Brett has begun modeling himself after his father, repeating Joe Camber's phrases, attitudes, and physical mannerisms; he has moved into the adult world of time-consciousness, simultaneously losing his innocence, and in that sense is safe. Gary Pervier has spent years trying to die; Joe Camber stands between Brett and the boy's future. They too die. But attention focuses on Tad Trenton. Although King has frequently disavowed intentional symbolism in characters' names, <u>Tad</u>, like <u>Todd</u> in "Apt Pupil," reflects the German <u>Tod</u>, "death." If <u>Cujo</u> is an "Unconquerable force" (Warner), then Tod becomes the object against which that force expends itself, temporarily at least.

To consider these points is not to digress into symbolical readings or psychological suppositions. It is merely to say that in reading <u>Cujo</u>, one becomes aware of an odd kind of logic, of a progression of theme and imagery that parallels the progression of events. That Tad must die is not so much inevitable as realistic; sometimes such things happen. Youth dies and frustrated, discouraged adults must carry on. The final paragraphs of the novel, the coda restoring peace and meaning to Castle Rock, turns the reader further and further away from the tragedy of Tad's death to the reconciliation between Vic and Donna, to the renewed hope Charity Camber feels for Brett, and to Cujo himself, with a brief, final glance at the rabbit's bones lying undisturbed forever.

Cujo is a fascinating, painful novel. It reaches out beyond itself to touch other of King's works: The Dead Zone, The Stand, Christine and The Talisman; "The Reach" and "The Raft"; and most significantly, Rage, Roadwork, and Thinner. Charity Camber's reactions to men's hunting trips re-creates a crucial scene from Rage; Althea Breakstone's disintegration following the death of her son not only foreshadows Donna's collapse at the end of Cujo but echoes Mary Dawes' in Roadwork. When Donna appears wearing white shorts and a red blouse, King adumbrates the "uniform" that appears in Thinner (39, 40, 187, 299). The latter connections are understandable; as King's agent, Kirby McCauley, says: "Steve thought of Cujo as more of a Bachman book. There was nothing supernatural about it, and it certainly had a downbeat ending" (Brown).

Cujo remains ambiguous and ambivalent. At times it evokes the visceral reactions associated with horror fiction; Debra Stump argues that Tad's death helps keep Cujo "within the genre" (136). Yet it constantly de-emphasizes the supernatural, allowing connections between Cujo, Frank Dodd, and the monster in the closet to remain as tenuous as possible.

In The Dead Zone (1979), King's directions seem clearer. Although preceding Cujo by two years, it fits logically after Cujo in a discussion of King's treatment of the supernatural. Cujo leaves the question open; The Dead Zone answers and explains.

There are, of course, additional connections between the two, primarily the presence of Frank

50

Dodd. Although both Douglas Winter (<u>Art</u> 97) and
Leonard Heldreth (146-147) have noted that King
added the references to Dodd in a later draft of
<u>Cujo</u>, the decision to cross-reference with <u>The
Dead Zone</u> helped establish the later novel even
more clearly as King's "first attempt at exceeding
the traditional limits of the horror genre"
(Stump, "A Matter of Choice" 131). The realism of
character, setting, and action King develops in
<u>The Dead Zone</u> spills over into <u>Firestarter</u> and
<u>Cujo</u>, endowing them with greater objectivity and
possibility and shifting them closer to science
fiction or mainstream literature than to horror.
     Reading (or re-reading) <u>The Dead Zone</u> con-
firms King's strength in characterization. Although many of the episodes seem incredible, the
characters are not. By dedicating more space to
minor characters than many writers might dare,
King allows Johnny Smith (the archetypal "common
man") and the others to develop beyond the pages.
Readers can empathize with their struggles and
fears to a degree unusual even in King. The final
passage, as Sarah intuits Johnny's presence in the
cemetery, is particularly strong, since the reader
has participated deeply in the loves, lives, and
losses of both. The resolution is not perfect,
but it is the best one can expect in an imperfect
world.
     King's emphasis on character explains much of
the novel's attraction. Douglas Winter (<u>RG</u> 75),
Fritz Leiber (<u>FI</u>), Alan Warren (23) and others,
have discussed <u>The Dead Zone</u> as among King's
finest novels, if not <u>the</u> finest. Such a claim
demands support, and the support is not long in
coming. <u>The Dead Zone</u> is one of King's most
restrained works, handling both the everyday and
the paranormal with extraordinary skill, weaving
empathy with interest, action with engagement, and
avoiding a too-frequent use of King's characteristic scatological language. And, as Leiber says,
it does so without relying on supernatural elements as short-cuts to reader interest. <u>The
Shining</u> would be a very different novel without
the malevolence King attributes to the Overlook;
<u>The Dead Zone</u> could succeed without any reference
to the supernatural at all, merely on the strength
of its clear, precise characterization.
     In fact, King goes out of his way to deny the

51

supernatural in The Dead Zone, just as he would do in Cujo. In Cujo everything could be explained through rabies and coincidence. Even the connections with Frank Dodd, or Vic and Donna Trenton's eerie experiences in Tad's closet could result from hallucination, hyper-sensitivity, or other psychological quirks.

In The Dead Zone, King moves even further from the supernatural. True, Johnny Smith does have an ability beyond most human experience, but it is treated in the novel as paranormal rather than abnormal. Weizak casts his explanation of Johnny's state in technical, scientific terminology. "You may also quote me as saying," he tells the assembled journalists," that this man is now in possession of a very new human ability, or a very old one." Johnny's damaged brain limits him but also opens new perceptions, not easily understood perhaps but still explainable:

> another tiny part of John Smith's brain appears to have awakened. A section of the cerebrum within the parietal lobe. This is one of the deeply grooved sections of the 'forward' or 'thinking' brain. The electrical responses from this section of Smith's brain are way out of line from what they should be, nuh? Here is one more thing. The parietal lobe has something to do with the sense of touch--how much or how little we are not completely sure--and it is very near to that area of the brain that sorts and identifies various shapes and textures. And it has been my own observation that John's "flashes" are always preceded by some sort of touching. (Ch. 11, pt. 2)

The point here is not the validity of King's science; perhaps this passage is more of what Michael Demarest calls "pseudoscientific hokum" in Firestarter. What is important is that in the context of the novel, Johnny Smith's actions and abilities receive careful, rational explanation based on scientific observation and expressed in scientific language. No matter how extraordinary the manifestation of those abilities, King constantly returns to physiological causes: brain trauma, either from the accident or from the skating incident when Johnny was a child.

More than anything else, this element of the novel differentiates it from what many readers consider archetypal Stephen King. There are no monsters in The Dead Zone. Or rather, the monsters are only too obviously human: cruel and manipulative types like Greg Stillson, Sonny Elliman, or Richard Dees, the representative of Inside View (an ironic title, in light of Johnny's ability); unthinking mobs led by demagogues; or simply insensitive people carried away by situations, as with those who beg Johnny to locate missing relatives without realizing how deeply it hurts him to handle a scarf from a dead man. Yet even their deviousness, their callousness, and their insensitive curiosity are clearly human; it requires no crossing into the supernatural for most of the characters to remain believable.

In addition, The Dead Zone moves beyond Cujo in its sense of threat. Cujo, frightening as he may be (and that is frequently inordinately so), is still only a dog. He kills four people and injures one more before he is killed. The tragedy is local and personal, warranting only brief mention in the newspapers.

The Dead Zone begins that way, but quickly expands its focus. Johnny Smith's first manifestations of his new ability are equally local and private. He knows that Marie Michaud's boy will respond well to surgery; he knows that Weizak's mother is alive; he tells Sarah where to find her lost wedding ring. With Eileen Magown, however, his ability expands beyond the personal level. Her home is threatened by fire, an external, destructive force circumvented by Johnny's newly developed ability. As The Dead Zone progresses, Johnny's influence widens, becoming increasingly important. By identifying the Castle Rock killer, he potentially saves the lives of a number of women. By convincing Chuck Chatsworth not to attend the graduation party, he saves scores of lives even though seventy-five young people die. And by stopping Stillson's election, he may have averted a global catastrophe.

The transition from private and internal to public and external defines the increasing com-

plexity of The Dead Zone. Winter's analysis of
the novel in Art concentrates on the Jekyll-Hyde
manifestations of evil, beginning with Johnny
Smith's grotesque Halloween mask as symbol of
potential, internal evil, expanding to include the
wheel of fortune as symbol of external evil, and
culminating in Greg Stillson's identification with
the laughing tiger: a man beneath the tiger suit,
and beneath the man a beast (70-73). Even beyond
the overtly symbolic imagery, however, The Dead
Zone couples the suggestion of visceral horror
present in such vivid images as Frank Dodd's
murders and suicide or Greg Stillson's bloody destruction of the dog in the Prologue, with a
consistent realism of setting and characterization.

The Dead Zone is also an intensely personal
novel. Written between 1976 and 1977, at a time
when King was having difficulty writing (Winter,
Art 76), it reflects a number of personal elements. Vera Smith's death carries the same power
as in Roadwork or the death scene in "The Woman in
the Room," both conscious connections with King's
mother; the relationship between mother and son in
the fictions gains strength by echoing King's
experiences.

More positively, early in The Dead Zone,
Johnny Smith is approached by David Bright, a re-
porter from the Bangor Daily News. Initially interested primarily in Smith as a recovered coma
victim, Bright covers the story of Eileen Magown's
house and is also present at the disastrous tele-
vised interview that results in Vera Smith's heart
attack and death. Unlike Roger Dussault or, later
in the novel, Richard Dees, David Bright is an
honest, responsible newsman uninterested in sensationalism or manipulation of the news.

Although a minor character in The Dead Zone,
Bright is important as a connection between fiction and life. While at UMO, King wrote for The
Maine Campus, then edited by David Bright. In the
"Garbage Truck" columns, King refers to Bright: to
his courageous responses to harrassment during the
march to end the war (15 May 1969); to his friend-
ship (8 August 1969); to his expertise as editor
(30 October 1969); and as one of King's candidates
for "Gutsiest Student Body Members" in the final
"Birth Announcement" column (21 May 1970). By in-

cluding Bright in <u>The Dead Zone</u> under his own name
and as a journalist, King accentuates the realistic tone of the novel.

Similarly, a brief reference to Harrison
Beach (Ch. 1, part 4) echoes King´s early poem
"Harrison State Park ´68" (1968), with its oblique
references to violent death, as well as Harrison
College in <u>Firestarter</u> (1980). Again, these
touches subtly reinforce the strength of <u>The Dead
Zone</u> by giving the novel outside referents; it
exists not only as an isolated fiction but also in
relation to other fictions and to external experience.

<u>The Dead Zone</u>, like <u>Cujo</u>, may be atypical,
given what many readers expect from Stephen King.
It is, however, one of his strongest novels, com-
pelling in movement and in depicting the unrest of
the seventies, forceful in style and execution,
and convincing in characterization--without relying on supernatural horror to generate interest.

After completing <u>The Stand</u>, King felt written
out. He finished "Rita Hayworth and Shawshank
Redemption" (<u>DS</u> 1982), then began <u>The Dead Zone</u>.
Part way through, he set the manuscript aside and
started <u>Firestarter</u>. After drafting about a third
of <u>Firestarter</u>, he returned to <u>The Dead Zone</u>; the
two novels were written almost simultaneously, a
fact that helps explain similarities between them,
the most important for this discussion being their
attitudes toward the interaction of the natural
and the supernatural.

In an interview with Douglas Winter in January, 1984, King commented on thematic parallels
between <u>Firestarter</u> and <u>Carrie</u> and on the probable
reaction of critics to those parallels. As a
genre writer, he would undoubtedly be accused of
self-imitation:

> I thought that critics might claim that
> Steve King had started to eat himself;
> but I recognized that they would do no
> such thing if I were a "serious" novel-
> ist--they would say, as you have, that
> Stephen King is attempting to amplify
> themes that are intrinsic to his work.
> And, with that in mind, I made my peace
> with <u>Firestarter</u>. (<u>Art</u> 76)

55

King's responses are doubly important. First,
they define the disparity King sees between his
treatment as a novelist and the treatment afforded
to "serious" (i.e., mainstream) novelists. And
second, they establish connections between Firestarter and Carrie.
  Both perceptions are helpful in assessing
Firestarter. On the surface, it seems, as King
feared, to repeat elements of Carrie: a young girl
has unusual powers which, when unleashed, destroy
everything around her. While writing the episode
on the Mander's farm, King says in the interview,
he became convinced that the parallels were too
close, and subsequently set the novel aside.
  Yet after working on The Dead Zone, he returned to the manuscript, re-read it, and decided
that it not only differed from Carrie but improved
upon the earlier novel (Winter, Art 76).
  In part the difference lies in King's treatment of Charlie McGee's powers. As with Johnny
Smith's powers in The Dead Zone, King bases her
pyrokinesis on a scientific premise--or at least
creates the illusion of scientific support.
Michael Demarest refers to her "napalm-to-nuclear
capabilities" and her "inflammatory forte" (K18);
the trivial tone in these phrases, and in the review as a whole, parallels Demarest's attitude toward the novel. After summarizing the results of
the Shop's experiments (Vicky develops telekinesis, Andy "comes off the couch" able to dominate
minds), Demarest says:

>   The drug has changed both parents' chro-
>   mosomal structure: it is this mutation,
>   not convincingly explained by King, that
>   has produced Charlie's pyrokinesis.
>   (K12)

Demarest may refer slightingly to King's basing
the novel on at least a "pseudoscientific" suppo-
sition; what he misses is the importance of that
attempt. It would have been easy enough for King
merely to have asserted pyrokinesis; after all, in
'Salem's Lot, vampires simply appear, as supernatural phenomena simply occur throughout the horror
literature as a genre.
  King's insistence that the McGees' abilities
lie outside the range of normal human experience

yet fit within the reality we accept as normal transforms _Firestarter_ from just another horror novel about a haunted child into something more closely approximating what King achieved in _The Dead Zone_ and _Cujo_, the two novels bracketing _Firestarter_. If, as his comments to Winter suggest, King was concerned about the different critical standards applied to genre writers and to mainstream writers, these three novels may have been in part a response to that disparity. While appealing to his reader's taste for horror, the three also define their characters, settings, and actions as possible within our objective, scientifically oriented universe.

There are, of course, contradictory elements in _Firestarter_ as there were in _The Dead Zone_ and _Cujo_. Certain scenes compel a visceral reaction consonant with supernatural horror. When one of Andy McGee's "pushes" becomes a "lethal ricochet" and Herm Pynchot shoves his arm into a garbage disposal unit, committing grisly, bloody suicide, Andy responds with "horror . . . and there was a caveman who capered and rejoiced." Throughout, as Winter notes, the novel concentrates on widening circles of paranoia and fear, on a "pursuit and confrontation pattern native to the espionage novel" (_Art_ 77), it also depicts increasingly dangerous potentials of Charlie's powers. While her mother could only absent-mindedly close refrigerator doors and her father could at most "push" a few people into greater self-confidence, Charlie possesses more frightening powers. At first, she too restricts her actions to individuals or small, non-threatening manifestations: she sets fire to the chauvinistic soldier's shoes and steals coins from telephone booths. Later, as the chase intensifies, she must expand the limits of her power, destroying men and machines until finally Wanless describes her as having the potential to split the earth itself "like a china plate in a shooting gallery."

Balancing these assertions of the horrific, however, are King's repeated and insistent connections between the McGees' powers and scientific research. Throughout the novel, he explains their apparently supernatural abilities; and, as in _The Dead Zone_, the question of whether or not the explanations are sufficient is secondary to the role those explanations play in creating verisimilitude in the novel. Even Charlie's unwillingness to use her power is defined in terms of psychological conditioning--although underlying it is King's insistence that good characters in his novels rarely instigate action; they are more frequently acted upon (Winter 78). He chooses to clothe his thematic and moral purposes in the garb of scientific, explainable phenomena, even having Wanless make a symbolic connection between the fictional Charlie McGee and the historical John Milton, reinforcing the sense of Charlie's world as ours.

There is horror in <u>Firestarter</u>--and fear and terror, as de Laurentiis' recent film graphically shows. But there is also more, as there was more in <u>Carrie</u>, <u>The Dead Zone, and Cujo</u>. All four approach the boundaries of mainstream fiction, at times bridging the gap between it and genre fiction.

King follows a similar pattern in many of his short stories. In addition to the three stories from <u>Different Seasons</u>, "The Woman in the Room," and "The Last Rung on the Ladder," others focus on the horror implicit in this world: "Cain Rose Up," with its crazed killer; "The Man Who Loved Flowers," with its exploration of perverted sexuality and murder; "Man With a Belly," a study in meaningless circles of retribution; "Morning Deliveries," which blends pastoral settings with covert madness; "Suffer the Little Children," which allows for two equally possible explanations, madness or the supernatural, but does not force either on the reader; "Survivor Type," with its naturalistic account of self-cannibalism; and "The Wedding Gig," which avoids the supernatural entirely in its tale of a monstrous bride. (See <u>SW</u>.)

In other narratives, however, King begins with a realistic or naturalistic presentation, then shifts into the supernatural. In both "The Reach" (1981) and <u>Thinner</u> (1984), for example, he works through the possibilities inherent in this world before reaching out to touch the inexplicable. Stella Flanders achieves a life-like power early in "The Reach," long before King suggests the presence of ghosts and, through the metaphor of Stella crossing the frozen reach, allows the reader to cross unseen boundaries between this and other worlds (SW 166-170). This tension between the seen and the unseen, between the rational and the irrational, and the culminating resolution admitting both makes "The Reach" one of King's most satisfying fictions.

With Thinner, the transition is more obvious, and for that reason the novel provides an ideal bridge between this chapter and the one following. In spite of the asserted, visual horror of the opening paragraph, the novel actually begins within the world of objective and explainable phenomena. Billy Halleck, his wife, his friends, and his doctor all work through a list of possibilities to explain his weight loss: nervousness, excessive dieting, anorexia nervosa, herpes, heart irregularities, and even that ultimate, pervasive "horror" in King's fiction, cancer. Only after exhausting all rational explanations does Halleck accept the irrational--that he has been cursed.

Even then, King tempers the manifestation of supernatural horror with realism. There are in fact two curses in Thinner. Taduz Lemke touches Halleck's cheek, and mysteriously Halleck loses weight. In turn, Halleck curses Lemke and the gypsy band with the curse of the white man from the city; it is a pragmatic curse, firmly rooted in the historical attitude of city-dwellers toward transients, and embodied by Ginelli. When Ginelli attacks the camp with poison, guns, and threats against Lemke and his family, the curse is fulfilled--without any supernatural intervention. By the end of Thinner, King has balanced the two elements. On the one hand, Halleck faces death caused by a potassium and electrolyte imbalance in his system--a scientific explanation for the outcome of the gypsy curse. On the other, he receives the pulsating pie, as nauseatingly horrific an image as any in King. In addition, settings and descriptions combine to emphasize both the realistic and the supernatural. A glimpse of Halleck is sufficient to give a boy nightmares, just as his presence turns the boardwalk into a carnival freak show. (See also SK/RB 115-137.)

With Thinner, King extends the progression explored in Carrie, The Dead Zone, Firestarter and Cujo to its logical limits and beyond. When the gypsy curse is spoken, King crosses from the

59

twilight lands of possibilities into the world of
the supernatural; before us now lie the realms of
vampires, ghosts, and monsters . . . another facet
of the imagination of Stephen King.

Chapter V

"GHOULIES AND GHOSTIES"

The Shining, 'Salem's Lot,
Cycle of the Werewolf, Pet Sematary

Reading the works of Stephen King frequently
calls to mind an old Scottish invocation:

> From ghoulies and ghosties
> And long-legged beasties
> And things that go bump in the night,
>   Good Lord deliver us!

In spite of King's frequent forays into mainstream
and near-mainstream fictions, there are sufficient
"things that go bump in the night" in his works to
satisfy the most compulsive craving for horror.
And, again in spite of his demonstrated ability to
entertain and engage readers without resorting to
things horrific or supernatural, King is best
known for these explorations of the supernatural,
even though only a few of his novels and marginally more of his short stories involve what might be
considered "traditional" horror creatures: ghosts,
vampires, werewolves, etc.
    While King is aware of the background and
heritage of horror (see Indick, "Literary Tradition"), his works transform that heritage into a
presentation uniquely Stephen King's, uniquely appropriate for his contemporary readers. Part of
his inordinate appeal stems from his ability to
make horror seem possible, if not probable, within
the context of his readers' experiences; only occasionally, as in the two mens' club tales, "The
Man Who Would Not Shake Hands" and "The Breathing
Method," or in a work of conscious pastiche, as in
"Crouch End," does he evoke the language, struc-
ures, and effects of another age.   Early in his

career, he advised beginners trying to break into
the men´s magazine horror market that prospective
writers must

> Throw away Poe and Lovecraft before you
> start. . . . Both of these fine writers
> were rococo stylists, weaving words into
> almost Byzantine patterns. . . .
>   A great many writers begin with the
> mistaken notion that "the Lovecraft
> style" is essential to success in the
> field. Those who feel this way no doubt
> pick up the idea by reading the numerous
> Lovecraft-oriented anthologies on sale.
> But anthologies are not magazines, and
> while the idea is no small tribute to
> H.P.L.´s influence on the field, it´s
> simply not so. If you´re looking for
> alternatives (ones that are adaptable to
> the men´s magazine format), I´d recom-
> mend John Collier, Richard Matheson,
> Robert Bloch (who began as a Lovecraft
> imitator and has made a successful
> switch to a more modern style), and Har-
> lan Ellison. All of these writers have
> short story anthologies on the market,
> and a volume of each makes a wonderful
> exercise book for the beginner. ("Market
> Writer and the Ten Bears" 11-12)

More commonly, King takes his own advice and
welds contemporary style, structures, images, and
attitudes onto the traditional forms, with the result that his fictions both partake of and transform what has gone before. "Dolan´s Cadillac,"
for instance, is at once recognizably influenced
by Poe´s "The Cask of Amontillado," yet unequivo-
cably Stephen King in its extended descriptions,
its concentration on visceral responses to pain
and grief, and its self-conscious cross-referenc-
ing with King´s own fiction. Only rarely does he
present substantially unaltered representations of
conventional horrors; more frequently, he either
transmogrifies them to suit his narrative purposes
or constructs his own inimitable brand of "creature": the inexplicable black thing in "The Raft";
Richie Grenadine in "Gray Matter," transformed
through some process that defies definition into a

thing that defies description; or the sand-entity
in "Beachworld," which suggests science fiction
(i.e., Stanislaw Lem's sentient ocean in Solaris)
while equally asserting horror fantasy. Still,
his fiction occasionally allows the "ghosties and
ghoulies" of traditional supernatural horror to
peek through.

Ghosts and Hauntings

With the exception of the invisible staff and
guests at the Overlook Hotel in The Shining, the
execrable but largely undeveloped Roland Le Bay in
Christine (about whom more in a later chapter),
the image of Hubie Marsten hanging from the raf-
ters of the Marsten House in 'Salem's Lot, and a
hint of ghostly presence in The Stand (786-789),
King's novels do not concentrate on that staple of
the supernatural horror, the ghost.

To move into the realm of the ghostly, readers are better served by King's short stories.
"The Reach" touches only the outer fringes of that
ghostly landscape, looking more toward this life
than to the next. The ghostly presences Stella
Flanders meets are but extensions of what she has
known for nearly a century in her isolation on
Goat Island; their voices are gentle and warm and
sing of love, a repeated motif in Skeleton Crew
(SW 166-170). The ghosts do not frighten; they
invite. Like Conrad Aiken's "silent snow, secret
snow," they whisper peace.

Similarly, while "Squad D" may be considered
a "ghost story" of sorts, it entails an intrigu-
ingly compassionate haunting: a figure mysteriously appears in a photograph, reuniting comrades in
arms and bringing resolution and an initially uncomfortable peace to families disrupted by the
Viet Nam conflict. In spite of the presence of
suicide and death, both stories are oddly optimistic and upbeat; in neither case do the "ghosts"
resemble the ectoplasmic entities of traditional
tales.

This does not mean, however, that King is incapable of creating, or uninterested in, ghosts
that rant or ghosts that threaten. While "Nona"
is in part an exercise in the psychology of horror
and madness, it can also be interpreted as a
rather traditional ghost story, complete with the

appurtenances associated with nineteenth century
ghosts: a graveyard, a white mausoleum, an empty
bier with "withered rose petals . . . scattered
across it like an ancient bridal offering," and
the final, horrifying vision of the decaying body
ripped open and exposed, as if "turned into a
womb" (SC 356). The sexuality present in many
ghost stories (including the sublimated and repressed sexuality of James's The Turn of the
Screw) here becomes foremost; the narrator is sex-
ually obsessed and repressed, uncomfortable with
his own masculinity and threatened by the feminin-
ity he translates into images of rats and spiders.
"Nona" not only frightens through its supernatural
elements but threatens with its re-construction of
madness.

More ambiguously, King works directly with
revenants in "Sometimes They Come Back," defining
Vinnie Corey, Robert Lawson, and David Garcia as
ghosts, as malevolent in their own way as Nona.
In addition, however, King includes a complication
when Jim Norman conjures the Wayne-thing--not
quite a ghost, possibly a demon, certainly a
threat. When it arrives, "the air became heavier.
There was a thickness in it that seemed to fill
the throat and the belly with gray steel" (NS
172). It speaks with a voice unlike Wayne's, and
when the three attack the Wayne-thing and wither
away, it "seemed to melt and run together. The
eyes went yellow, and a horrible, grinning malig-
nancy looked out at him" (NS 175). Even though
the Wayne-thing had helped Jim Norman rid the
world of three evil presences, it remains, a shadow and a threat.

Ben P. Indick has referred to The Shining as
"Stephen King's consummate ghostly tale" ("Literary Tradition" 183). It is certainly that . . .
and much more. While ghosts aplenty inhabit the
corridors and suites of the Overlook Hotel, King
often draws attention away from the ghosts to the
Hotel itself. It is, with Shirley Jackon's The
Haunting of Hill House (King admires both the novel and the film version, by the way), an archetypal haunted house. Yet the Overlook differs
greatly from the austere and lonely Hill House
with its upright walls, neat bricks, firm floors
and doors "sensibly shut":

silence lay steadily against the wood
and stone of Hill House, and whatever
walked there, walked alone" (3)

The Overlook, on the other hand,

> was having one hell of a good time.
> There was a little boy to terrorize, a
> man and his woman to set one against the
> other, and if it played its cards right
> they could end up flitting through the
> Overlook's halls like insubstantial
> shades in a Shirley Jackson novel, what-
> ever walked in Hill House walked alone,
> but you wouldn't be alone in the Over-
> look, oh no, there would be plenty of
> company here. (281)

In addition, King blends motifs from other
literatures with the ghost story and the haunted-
house story. The Shining has its share of monsters: the topiary animals, not quite ghosts yet
as dependent as the ghosts upon the malevolent
sentience controlling the Overlook for their temporary life; the black thing in the playground,
again not quite defined as a ghostly manifestation; and the Jack-thing, the walking dead that
Jack becomes when the Overlook enters him and uses
his physical body to attack Danny.

Picking up threads from the Gothic tradition,
King includes a contemporary version of the Gothic
castle, isolated among lowering and "sublime"
mountain peaks and staffed by a full complement of
unsavory, supernatural inhabitants ("Every big
hotel has got a ghost"), threatening and brooding,
inviting to Jack Torrance's flawed Byronic character. And, true to his Gothic backgrounds, King
incorporates premonitions and dreams, both true
and false, most emphatically in the figure of
Tony, a vague manifestation of Danny's own perceptions; Danny's full name, after all, is Daniel
Anthony Torrance. Madness is similarly a consistent threat throughout, as each of the main characters questions his or her sanity in the face of
clearly irrational, inexplicable occurrences.
King never forgets, however, that fear of madness
is a last resort of rational minds, an ironic vestige of normality. In The Shining, the problem is

less madness than the simple fact that the Overlook is, in spite of all rationality, haunted and
haunting. Stanley Kubrick´s film of The Shining
errs by insisting on Jack Torrance´s madness; too
much in the film could be explained as a result of
Jack´ insanity and its effects on Danny´s sensi-
tive imagination. King, on the other hand, places
the Overlook at the center; his novel concerns
ghosts and hauntings, avoiding the "easy" ration-
alistic explanation of insanity.

King also weaves references to fairy tales
into the narrative, but fairy tales of the darker
sort--a technique Peter Straub would later expand
in Shadowland (chapter 4 of The Shining is in fact
called "Shadowland"). In an inversion of "Little
Red Riding Hood," for example, King makes the
grandmother the object of horror. In spite of
Tony´s warnings and Danny´s own understanding that
the Overlook threatens himself and his father,
Danny chooses to remain; the alternative is to
visit grandmother´s house and confront a contemporary monster which, like the wolf in the tale,
wants to eat Danny and Wendy (201-202). Later, as
Danny confronts more archaic terror in a haunted
room, he recalls a fairy tale his drunken father
once told him and couples it with his perception
of his grandmother: "what big teeth you have
grandma and is that a wolf in a BLUEBEARD suit or
a BLUEBEARD in a wolf suit . . ." (214). If one
accepts Eric S. Rabkin´s psychological interpretation of "Little Red Riding Hood" as admonishing
its listeners about the dangers of maturation (37-
38), the relationship of the fairy tale to Danny
Torrance becomes even more critical; like Red
Riding Hood, he too must ultimately face danger
alone, isolated from adult support yet trapped in
a world the adults have created (unless--drawing
the analogy perhaps too far--Hallorann is seen as
the hunter-figure who rescues Danny at the last
moment). As with so many of King´s young characters, Danny Torrance is forced to act older, more
responsibly than his years would normally allow
since even fairy tales turn against Danny, joining
with the Overlook to weave a tighter texture of
terror.

In spite of King´s momentary excursions into
fairy tale, however, the Overlook is haunted;
when, at the end, Hallorann sees a monstrous dark

shape escaping through the blasted windows of the
Presidential suite, looking like a "huge, obscene
manta" before scattering to the winds, King implies that something had possessed the Overlook
and brought the ghosts and topiary animals to life
even as it destroyed Jack Torrance . . . and has
now escaped. Since evil is frequently external to
characters, coming in its own time and through its
own will, it cannot be destroyed; the best King's
characters can hope for is a temporary victory in
a single, isolated skirmish. As in ´Salem´s Lot,
The Shining, The Stand, Christine, Pet Sematary,
The Eyes of the Dragon, The Talisman; and so many
of King´s short stories, the horrific elements,
though displaced, survive, and in their survival
lies the kernel of future horror.

There is more to The Shining than this complex of horror motifs, however. The novel often
refers to mainstream writers--poets, novelists,
playwrights--as well as to fairy tales and fantasies. The result is a richly textured narrative, allusive and elusive. Poe´s "The Masque of
the Red Death" provides a recurrent, crucial image, while King´s references to Lewis Carroll´s
Alice in Wonderland juxtapose horror with lighter
fantasy, punning on Carroll´s title; for Danny
Torrance, the rabbit hole signals his entry into a
"land full of sick wonders" (306). Balancing the
fantasies of Poe and Carroll, however, Jack Torrance refers to Sean O´Casey´s plays as models for
his own (104, 105); a dozen pages later, King
makes what might be a similar pun on the title of
O´Casey´s Purple Dust as he describes Danny´s
"huge purple Volkswagon" as "burning up a dirt
track" (116). Emily Dickinson´s "A Narrow Fellow
in the Grass" contributes the image of Jack "all
zero at the bone" (127), connecting the continuing
serpent/snake imagery with the increasingly important and threatening snow, while at the same time
tying The Shining at least temporarily to mainstream American literature.

King´s allusions to mainstream literary figures also function structurally as a parallel to
one of the most intriguing developments in The
Shining. In addition to King´s typical references
to contemporary politics (Nixon, Rockefeller, Ford
and others), King concentrates on allusions to the
theater, working throughout the novel to create an

extended metaphor based on plays. He mentions
such theatrical celebrities as Jean Harlow, Clark
Gable, Marilyn Monroe, Carole Lombard, and Robert
Redford; films such as Ray Milland´s The Lost
Weekend, an appropriate connection; and, more importantly, playwrights: Sean O´Casey, Arthur Miller, Eugene O´Neil, Shakespeare, T. S. Eliot.

After all, Jack Torrance is a playwright--or
is trying to become such. And The Little School,
which he is working on, reflects his own life in
setting and characterization: he must eventually
"school" both himself and his family (as Delbert
Grady once schooled his). As a result, The Shining becomes an involved, convoluted exploration of
play in multiple senses, in the importance of
words and their relationship to reality. Again
and again King allows Jack to refer to "his" play
in phrases that echo ambiguously throughout the
novel. Jack plans on finishing his play before
the New Year; it would be done by then, he hopes,
"for better or worse" (120). The Overlook com-
pletes its "play," literally a masque modeled on
Poe´s "Masque of the Red Death," between Thanks-
giving and Christmas--definitely for the worse.
During his disastrous telephone conversation with
Ullman, Jack comments that he hadn´t yet gotten
around to murdering his wife; he was "saving that
until after the holidays, when things get dull"
(178). Later, as the Overlook insinuates itself
more completely into Jack´s will, he re-reads his
play, discovering that it no longer reflects his
view of reality. His loyalties have shifted, as
has his conception of how the struggle must end,
with himself becoming more like the authority figure, Danny like the recalcitrant, rebellious student. The play parallels life at the Overlook;
and in a phrase foreshadowing the climax of the
novel, King notes that Jack Torrance was unable to
complete it. His attitudes toward himself, Wendy,
and Danny are as ambiguous and uncertain as his
attitudes toward his characters.

There is, of course, a reason for the cen-
trality of play as image in The Shining. In addition to the immediate symbolical and imagistic
value of play as mimesis, King uses drama--partic-
ularly tragedy--as a structural device. The novel
is divided into five parts, reflecting the five
acts of Shakespearean tragedy. "On The Shining

and Other Perpetrations" discusses his original conception for the novel explicitly in terms of Shakespearean tragedy, acts, and scenes, concluding with the comment that the project "probably sounds pretentious, and undoubtedly was" (14) but that the tragic structure created a sense of "staging" critical to the finished novel:

> The result was an incredibly strong sense of visualization for me, the writer, and that has apparently carried over to the book's readers, who seem to do more than simply dislike Mr. Kubrick's film of the book; they actually seem <u>offended</u> by it, or by Kubrick's concretization of the highly personal images with which the book provided them. (15)

The images in <u>The Shining</u> are indeed powerful: the wasps, with their pervasive sense of threat finally linked imagistically with the sentience of the Overlook itself; the topiary animals and the roque mallet, far more effective than Kubrick's substitutions; the elevator, carpet, and Presidential suite; the serpentine fire-hose, the image at the center of King's original idea for the novel and the one that formed the "bones of the book" ("On The Shining" 13). They remain with the reader, incrementally more powerful as King layers images with meaning after meaning, transforming them from the level of physical objects to increasingly symbolic devices. Even something as initially innocuous as a key becomes a powerful image when coupled with the blood-stained clock and the Poesque masque of death for which Danny functions as the key.

In keeping with the sense of novel as play, King also wrote an Epilogue and Prologue. Although they tied together many of the imagistic and narrative strands, the published novel would have been almost five hundred pages long had they been included. Accordingly, King deleted them on the advice of his editor at Doubleday. The Prologue, published later as "Before the Play," introduces many of the images and episodes alluded to in the novel; although interesting in itself, it is not entirely necessary to understanding <u>The</u>

69

Shining. The Epilogue has disappeared, except for
the final chapter of the published novel--Wendy,
Danny, and Hallorann in Maine, establishing order
and direction to their shattered lives.

On an even deeper level, however, The Shining
moves beyond the the motif of play reflecting life
to touch upon language itself. Words are critical
in the novel. Danny Torrance cannot read; Tony
shows him frustratingly incomprehensible signs,
and the recurrent "redrum" horrifies Danny primarily because of its meaninglessness. As Danny
learns to read and unlocks the secrets of words,
he understands more and more about the Overlook
and its threat. Jack, on the other hand, moves in
the opposite direction. Initially verbal, he
becomes increasingly averbal, morose and with-
drawn, unable to write, and finally, after the
Overlook possesses him almost entirely, restricted
in language to obscenities, scatological phrasing,
and barbarisms. He loses control over the words
that structure his reality, then loses that reality itself.

Hallorann similarly illustrates the importance of words. The "shine," after all, consists
in the ability to communicate directly, to send
words from one mind to another. As the novel approaches its climax, he loses contact with Danny,
receiving instead the message sent by the Overlook: not words, but "a series of rebuslike images," painful and potent (391-392). Even after
the boiler explodes and the great dark shadow
erupts from the window of the Presidential suite,
there is still danger. Searching for blankets in
the shed, Hallorann sees the roque mallets, then
receives a series of images: bone and blood juxtaposed with iced tea, swings, ladies in summer
hats, and the sound of mosquitoes. King signals
the danger Hallorann faces by transposing image
for word.

This undercurrent of symbolic meaning reinforces the purpose of The Shining as horror novel.
Horror, as King has so often pointed out, develops
when disorder intrudes upon order. In The Shining, characters repeatedly move from order to
chaos and back again, beginning with minor cycles
and culminating in a reaffirmation of rationality
and sanity. The final chapter seems anticlimactic
in its calmness yet is essential to the novel. In

spite of what has happened at the Overlook, the change of location as the characters return to King's Maine assures that there is still order somewhere.

The Shining is about ghosts; it is about a haunted house; and it is about gothic romanticism. Yet these generic considerations are secondary to King's obsession with order. Because of this, and because of its brilliant handling of plot, theme, setting, characterization, image, symbol--the appurtenances of literature--it is also among King's most teachable novels, touching readers on levels far divorced from ghosts and haunts.

Vampires

"In the early 1800's," King says in the "Garbage Truck" column for December 18, 1969, "a whole sect of Shakers, a rather strange religious persuasion at best, disappeared from their village (Jeremiah's Lot) in Vermont. The town remains uninhabited to this day."

In this comment lies two important elements in 'Salem's Lot (1975), "Jerusalem's Lot" (NS 1978), and "One for the Road" (1977): first, the distinctive name, Jerusalem's Lot, apparently derived in part from Jeremiah's Lot; and second, the specter of a town inexplicably deserted.

Working from these beginnings through an interest in how a vampire could survive in contemporary American society, King completed one of his favorite novels, 'Salem's Lot. His second published novel (originally titled Second Coming), 'Salem's Lot is also among his rarest as far as collectible trade editions go. Initially selling at $7.95, by 1983 first editions in good condition sold for between $350 and $450; as of August 1985, only a decade after publication, the same volumes might command between $500 and $650, with a "mint" (i.e., virtually unread) copy running as high as $750. The initial press run was relatively small for Doubleday, perhaps fewer than 5,000 and possibly smaller even than the press run for Carrie. In addition, although the novel reached the bestsellers lists (King's first appearance in hardcover), he was still comparatively unknown and not as obviously collectible as he would become; many copies probably disappeared through hard use and multiple readings. "No one seems to know why this particular book is so valuable," Peter Schneider concludes, however, adding that

> it is certainly no rarer than his first novel, <u>Carrie</u>, which goes for a good deal less. (This is borne out by the fact that first editions of <u>´Salem´s Lot</u> pop up in huckster rooms at conventions with the same regularity that H. P. Lovecraft´s <u>Necronomicon</u>, with only three or four copies reputedly in existence, appeared in innumerable "dark and accursed" libraries.) (2709)

The mention of Lovecraft´s name and fiction is appropriate in conjunction with <u>´Salem´s Lot</u>. The atmosphere surrounding Jerusalem´s Lot recalls Lovecraft´s backwoods New England, with its ramshackle buildings and eerily degenerate inhabitants. Not that King goes out of his way to echo Lovecraft; in fact, the first chapters of <u>´Salem´s Lot</u> are remarkably clear of such authorial borrowings. Alan Ryan provides a careful, detailed account of King´s narrative movement in the opening pages of the novel, beginning with the reference to Jackson´s Hill House as an introductory sketch for the Marsten House. "It is essential," he says, "that the Marsten House, from the first moment we lay eyes on it, be scary." King incrementally "predisposes" the reader to fear, Ryan continues, by controlling the pace of action as Ben Mears approaches the Lot, delaying as long as possible the first view of the House itself, then revealing its "peaked, gabled roof" in the climactic position at the end of the sentence and the paragraph (190).

While Ryan´s point is well taken, it is also important to note that King works--apparently with equal consciousness--at disallowing any particular sense of horror or dread this early in the novel. The atmosphere is curiously diffuse, the elements of fear and terror hidden for the most part in Ben Mears´ memories, which he divulges only much later. Weaving through hints of things desperately wrong we see the landscape of King´s Maine: the "grand final fling" of summer countering Mears´ "not unpleasurable tingle of excitement in his

belly" (13). A near accident with a motorcycle
unnerves Mears--for no immediately apparent rea-
son--and then dissolves in a "burst of pleasure
and recognition" as he spots a familiar red barn.
Again and again, King volleys between images of
fear and images of pleasure, delaying the moment
when his narrative passes irrevocably into the
realm of horror fantasy.

The atmosphere gradually thickens, shadows
fall over the Lot, eerie and unspeakable events
occur (which King carefully does <u>not</u> graphically
define) until only one element remains hidden.

The vampire.

Even as perceptive a reader as Peter Straub
reacted with surprise to the description of Barlow
as Dud Rogers sees him: "My God! I thought: a
vampire! Nearly everything about this moment took
my breath away . . ." (8). The surprise, Straub
says, was well planned, well staged, well paced.
In a society surfeited with literary and cinematic
vampires, where over 600 film versions of vampires
have skulked across screens since the early 1900s
and uncountable paperback novels have exploited
every potential of the theme from the serious to
the parodic, to introduce a vampire at all requires courage.

Indeed, most of the more successful recent
revivifications of the vampire motif have altered
the formula to make it more palatable. Colin Wil-
son´s <u>The Space Vampires</u> (1976) is really about SF
alien invaders who consciously cloak themselves in
the paraphernalia of Bram Stoker´s <u>Dracula</u>. F.
Paul Wilson´s <u>The Keep</u> and Whitley Strieber´s <u>The
Hunger</u> both posit alternate non-human but sentient
species; the novels carefully incorporate and explain away most of the vampire lore. Somtow Such-
aritkul´s <u>Vampire Junction</u> (1984; as S. P. Somtow)
moves his vampire through time and space, transforming Timmy Valentine into a rock musician, teen
idol, arcade master, and vampire, finally settling
his hero in backwoods Idaho.

But in ´Salem´s Lot, King does not attempt
any such transformation. Barlow is a vampire,
pure and simple, arriving in the dead of night in
a wooden crate, bearing no history (other than
vague suggestions necessary to establish residence
in the Lot). As Stoker did with Count Dracula and
King would later do <u>Cycle of the Werewolf</u>, the ex-

ternal evil merely is. There are (and can be) no explanations.

In addition, of course, the novel carries King's distinctive trademarks: graphic descriptions (it is among his "bloodiest" novels); characteristic language, frequently intrusive and self-defeating; and characters working through their own levels of isolation and guilt. Ben Mears must face two "vampires" simultaneously; the external, physical Barlow, who threatens Mears' life, and the inner "vampire" of memory threatening to sap him of strength and vigor (in this sense, he seems a precursor to Straub's Miles Teagarden in If You Could See Me Now). Susan Norton faces similar estrangement from her parents and from Floyd Tibbets; she has chosen a new direction but the old does not want to let her go. Mark Petrie's case differs subtly; like so many children in King's fiction, he enjoys no inherent connection with his parents, but exists separately from them, with interests and fears and knowledge that they cannot share.

Even more typically, King creates and then destroys what seems an ideal family unit: Mears, Susan Norton, and Mark Petrie. It is clear from the start that Ben Mears and Susan Norton act as hero and heroine. It is equally clear that Ben and Mark will end up together; the prologue establishes that. Yet, as happens again and again in King's fiction, the triad is disrupted. Carrie White's father deserted his family, leaving Carrie with an unwholesome and fanatical mother; Wendy and Danny Torrance survive Jack's murderous attacks, to become a partial family under Hallorann's partial protection; in The Stand, The Dead Zone, Firestarter, Cujo, Christine, Pet Sematary, The Talisman, Roadwork, The Running Man, and Thinner--in virtually all of King's novels, in fact-- the same disruption occurs, resulting in different alignments of parents and child but always entailing fragmentation.

In 'Salem's Lot, this fragmentation occurs perhaps most obviously because we observe it while the ties are still being created. Susan is drawn to Ben Mears, but barely meets Mark before her death; as King said in an interview:

I began having serious doubts about that

74

character because I´d conceived of her as being a really independent Maine girl. I started to say to myself: "This girl is twenty-three years old and out of school--yet she´s still living with her parents and not working." Belatedly I had to get her out of that situation, and it wasn´t very long before I decided, "Well, I´ll kill her off." It gave me great satisfaction to get rid of her. And I also thought that the reader´s reaction would be: If Susan Norton can go, anybody can go. Nobody is protected. (Grant 20)

King´s pragmatic decision parallels his symbolic fragmentation of relationships--no one is safe in the Lot.

The central alliance between Ben and Mark forms abruptly, forced upon both by violence and terror. And behind the three lurk shadowy figures from the Lot, alternatively supportive and threatening: Mrs. Miller and her roomers; Mark´s parents; Floyd Tibbets, with his curious attack on Ben; Mabel Werts, the archetypal monstrous woman common throughout King´s works. Against this backdrop, the possibilities for relationships shine brightly--but with the coming of the vampire, all is lost. Gary William Crawford calls 'Salem´s Lot the "blackest of King´s works" (44). Whether it descends into greater darkness than Pet Sematary is debatable; but Crawford correctly notes that 'Salem´s Lot provides neither transcendence nor relief. At the end as at the beginning, there is only exhaustion and emptiness.

To this extent, 'Salem´s Lot seems closely allied to the films that influenced King during his childhood, to those films of the fifties that exploited the paranoia of the times. King´s vampire is curiously off-center in the novel; far more time is devoted to other characters, to townspeople who find themselves in terrifying situations at the hands of neighbors and former friends: Mark Petrie confronted by the spectre of Danny Glick suspended in the air outside his window; Charlie Rhodes rushing into the night, only to see his bus filled with familiar faces now drawn and white except for shadowed eyes and ruby

75

red lips; or Mabel Werts answering a friend's call for help and receiving a vampire into her home as she opens the door: "Glynis was standing there stark naked, her purse over her arm, grinning with huge, ravenous incisors. Mabel had time to scream, but only once" (393). The purse over the arm, with its suggestion of a mindless vestige of normality, may be the most horrifying image in the passage.

The same feeling pervades many films of the fifties. Don Siegel's original Invasion of the Body Snatchers (1956) builds a similar sense of unreality, paradoxically by means of its unrelenting realism of presentation. Neighbors are no different on the surface, but essentially changed. As with Ben Mears and Mark Petrie, the forces of change prove too great for Kevin McCarthy's character; in fact, the film version most frequently screened includes a revised ending far more optimistic than originally planned. The sense of total isolation and helplessness in Siegel's initial version was so overpowering that audiences rejected the film as first produced. Similarly, the external threats and overt hints of social paranoia in Jack Arnold's The Creature from the Black Lagoon (1954) or Gordon Douglas' Them! (1954) or Christian Nyby's The Thing (1951) reflect throughout 'Salem's Lot, as do the myriad treatments of the vampire as cinematic staple.

The novel as finally published was in fact toned down by King's editors. An especially gruesome passage involving rats disappeared from Cody's death scene, for example. But what remains certainly ranks among King's most effective in evoking visceral responses. In "Market Writer and the Ten Bears" (1973), King identified ten phobias or "bears" that create the most convincing horror:

   1. Fear of the dark
   2. Fear of squishy things
   3. Fear of deformity
   4. Fear of snakes
   5. Fear of rats
   6. Fear of closed-on spaces
   7. Fear of insects (especially spiders, flies, beetles)
   8. Fear of death
   9. Fear of others (paranoia)

10. Fear _for_ someone else

The list is neither exhaustive nor exclusive; it simply represents what King calls his "top ten." Nor are these "bears" nightmares of the "night-time variety"; instead, they are the "ones that hide just beyond the doorway that separates the conscious from the unconscious" (10).

In 'Salem's Lot, King opens that doorway as wide as he can, releasing virtually all ten of the "bears" in a flood over the reader--with the result that 'Salem's Lot is potentially one of King's most difficult works to read. Only the fact of its fantastic premise--that there really _are_ vampires--allows the reader to compartmental-ize and step away from the psychological and phys-iological manipulations King devises in the novel.

Of the many "ghosties and ghoulies and long legged beasties" King re-creates, his vampires, including as they do nearly everyone left behind in Jerusalem's Lot, remain the most vivid . . . and the most directly horrific.

One mark of the power inherent in 'Salem's Lot is that King has discussed possible sequels to it. While several of his novels invite sequels (the final paragraphs of Christine, for example, with the probability of yet another intrusion by the demon car into Dennis Guilder's life), he has specifically mentioned returning to the Lot. He has suggested that he might begin with Ben Mears and Mark Petrie and their joint decision to go back to the Lot and complete their task; alterna-tively, he has said that he might open with Father Callahan confronting his guilt and discovering a need to return to the Lot. In either case, the fact remains that 'Salem's Lot has cast as intri-cate and long-lasting a spell upon its creator as it has upon many of its readers.

Werewolves

We may tremble before the vampire; we may shudder at the ephemeral touch of the ghost; we may abhor the creature whose sole purpose is to wreak death and destruction.

But ultimately we pity the werewolf.

Where we might cheer the sight of Dracula disintegrating into dust or, as Frank Langella

77

did, spiraling into nothingness beneath the sun,
we frequently react more ambiguously to the death
of the werewolf. Whether it be Lon Chaney's
classic 1941 portrayal, or Michael Landon's teenage werewolf, or a more contemporary version
complete with bloodchilling special effects (David
Naughton's in An American Werewolf in London, for
example), the werewolf seems to inspire as much
pity as terror.

Unlike other creatures of horror, the werewolf is often more sinned against than sinning.
As Bill Pronzini aptly points out, the werewolf
differs from other creatures of myth or legend.
It is not created in the laboratory or one of the
walking undead; it is neither zombie nor mummy
preserved by tana leaves; it is not a vampire, a
witch, or a demon. Instead,

> "He is just a man, a woman, a mortal
> human being.
>   Who is cursed. (xiii)

The curse works in two ways. On the level of
plot, it transforms an otherwise sane, rational
individual into a ravening monster. More discon-
certingly, however, on the level of theme and symbol it divorces that individual from reality,
often arbitrarily isolating the afflicted person
from society at large and from personal standards
of morality and behavior. There frequently seems
to be no inherent reason why the victim succumbs
to the curse of the werewolf; it simply happens.
The victim may not be at fault and often struggles
valiantly against what is happening. Yet finally
the victim--and further victims besides--suffer
because of it.

Perhaps for this reason, of all the creatures
available to King as a horror writer, the werewolf
seems most alien to his temperament. The figure
appears only briefly in the novels, in the Oshkosh
overalled werebeasts in The Talisman, for example.
The one work devoted to the werewolf, Cycle of the
Werewolf, evolved almost as much by accident as
design. Cycle is unusual in King's canon for its
brevity and directness. As David Sherman says in
his review of the book,

> King is in fine (albeit abbrevi-

ated) form here, as space limitations
pare his storytelling abilities to their
bare essentials. Not having 400 pages
to wax literary in, he makes it short
and sweet. It´s like watching the All-
Star Game, and ace pitcher King only
gets to work one inning. He strikes out
the side, one-two-three; just enough of
a demonstration to remind everyone why
he´s the boss. (37)

Originally intended as a series of vignettes for a
calender with artwork by Bernie Wrightson, the
narrative gradually outgrew the conception, finally appearing in a hardcover edition (trade and
limited) from Land of Enchantment in 1983. As with
so many of King´s works, the price escalated dra-
matically, from an initial cover price of $28.50
to over $125 for the trade edition. Cost and in-
accessibility kept Cycle from wide distribution
until April 1985, when NAL/Signet brought out a
paperback trade edition, making the narrative
widely available for the first time. In his
review of the Land of Enchantment edition, David
Sherman concluded that "Cycle of the Werewolf is a
worthy investment . . . but wait ´till it hits the
discount bins before you invest" (37). Unfortunately for his prediction, and for would-be
buyers, the first editions of Cycle barely reached
retail outlets, let alone the discount bins.
    As one of King´s sparsest works, Cycle suc-
ceeds in spite of the fragmentation inherent in
the narrative structure, with essentially a different story for each month, told quickly and concentrating on only a few hours at most. Cycle is
an unusually moving piece, particularly when the
reader meets Marty Coslaw in July--halfway through
Cycle (even though King takes pains to connect
Marty retrospectively with January in the segment
for July, in part to suggest his presence throughout the year). Marty draws unusual empathy from
the reader, as King discovered when he completed
the narrative. Gradually, Marty took over, becoming the focus of attention before finally
ridding Tarker´s Mills of the werewolf. In fact,
King felt so strongly that Marty should have
emerged even sooner that his screenplay, Silver
Bullet, based on Cycle, ·moves Marty more into the

79

center where he belongs.

The emphasis on Marty Coslaw differentiates King's version of the werewolf motif from more traditional ones. More frequently, writers and storytellers concentrate on the werewolf, describing its backgrounds, eliciting both sympathy and empathy as the reader watches a normal man or woman inextricably destroyed by fate . . . or accident. As a result, readers are as much drawn to the werewolf's struggles against the curse when in the human state, as repulsed by its actions as a beast. The antithesis between the character's responses, symbolized by the shifting form, signals an ambivalence within the reader as well.

In Cycle, King de-emphasizes this ambiguity by shifting his focus first to the victims, then to Marty Coslaw. The Reverend Lester Lowe does not appear, even indirectly, until April, when the narrative is nearly a third completed--and then only in a single-line reference, along with half a dozen other inhabitants of Tarker's Mills. He first enters as a substantive character when he delivers his sermon in May, with its ironically symbolic title "The Beast Walks Among Us." In Lowe's subsequent dream, King dramatizes his theme of the evil within. In spite of several other minor references, King does not reveal Lowe's importance in the story until October, and only in November does Lowe admit to himself that "something is . . . well, wrong with him."

More critically, King never creates empathy for Lowe, as one might expect for the victim of the curse. Lowe remains a placid figure, delivering rather boring sermons, almost invisible in the community, his relation to the beast unsuspected by anyone except a single crippled boy--and Lowe is so parochial in outlook that he cannot even identify the one person who threatens his secret. When he decides in November to search out the threat, he speaks in curiously mixed terms, refusing even at this late point to accept his own role in what is happening. "Who was it in July?" he wonders. "It's time to find out." Calmly reading his newspaper, Lowe rationalizes that "All things serve the Lord's will, I'll find him. And silence him. Forever."

Because of his passivity, Lowe never engenders the empathy often associated with the were-

wolf; as a result, readers look elsewhere for a
focal point and find it in Marty Coslaw. A crip-
ple, Marty is isolated from his friends and from
his family. King emphasizes the mother's consistent brusqueness, the father's artificial "let's
be pals" attitude, and the sister's minor cruel-
ties that hide a deeper but inexpressible love.

In Tarker's Mills, love is at a premium, as
are other human relations. Each victim of the
werewolf expands the pervasive sense of isolation.
Arnie Westrum (January), the unknown drifter
(March), and the innocent but doomed youth Brady
Kinkaid (April) are isolated physically. Stella
Randolph (February) is isolated by her skewed romanticism and preoccupation with superficial
manifestations of love as well as by the
corpulence that makes her an object of ridicule in
Tarker's Mills. Constable Lander Neary (August)
ignores evidence that might have saved his own
life, retreating into the public image of the law
enforcement officer until it is too late. Milt
Sturmfuller (November) abuses his wife physically
and emotionally.

At the center, and most isolated of all,
Marty Coslaw becomes the focus for King's attention in Cycle. He is crippled, but King never
explains why or how. The cause is unimportant;
its effects on Marty's life, however, are. His
surviving the beast's first attack, his separation
from his family in the following months, his
discovery of the werewolf's identity, and his
decision to confront the beast only extend his
initial isolation. Even at the end, when Uncle Al
sits with him during the long night of the last
day of the year, he is in a sense alone. When
the beast attacks, Uncle Al watches, stunned and
unmoving, never firing the weapon he cradles in
his lap. Only Marty acts, shooting the beast
twice with the requisite silver bullets (the
silver coming from his melted-down confirmation
spoon).

Marty's disability and isolation are ultimately as much without rationale or justification
as the fact of the werewolf itself. "Something in-
human has come to Tarker's Mill," King says early
in "January":

as unseen as the full moon riding the

81

night sky high above. It is the werewolf, and there is no more reason for
its coming now than there would be for
the arrival of cancer, or a psychotic
with murder on his mind, or a killer
tornado. Its time is now, its place is
here . . . .

Nor does Lester Lowe have any better explanation
for what has occurred when he faces the truth in
"November": "This--whatever it is--is nothing I
asked for. I wasn´t bitten by a wolf or cursed by
a gypsy. It just . . . happened." The fact of
the werewolf remains as inexplicable as cancer or
psychosis or storm . . . or the paraplegia dis-
torting a young boy´s life.
     King does allow the image of the werewolf to
reflect externally humanity´s internal state. "The
beast within" is as critical in the narrative as
the one without, as when Marty sees something in
Lowe´s eyes on Halloween night, the bestial within
the human. Later, Lowe describes men hunting the
beast on the evening of the November full moon.
They enjoy the "chance to get out in the woods,
pull beers, piss in ravines, tell jokes about
polacks and frogs and niggers, shoot at squirrels
and crows," he says. "They´re the real animals."
     Cycle adds an interesting complexity to the
werewolf motif. It explores the man-beast, the
creature that metaphorically defines two sides of
human nature by separating them and giving each an
appropriate physical form. At the same time, however, it punctuates the meaninglessness and arbi-
trariness of such a division. In a world where
cancer can strike, where children die, where life
is at best tenuous, does not a werewolf (however
symbolically or metaphorically intended) effectively represent these external intrusions into
human existence. King´s were-beast both follows
the tradition and transcends it, symbolizing at
once inner and outer, internal human frailty and
external circumstantial evil.
     The publication of Signet´s softcover edition
of Cycle in April 1985 not only made the work more
accessible to King´s readers, but ameliorated two
important complaints. A number of reviewers
argued that while Cycle was interesting, it was
too lightweight to justify the initial cover

price. More seriously, the original edition con-
tained a number of typographical errors: "bloody"
instead of "bloody," "Pice" instead of "piece."
According to Edward Bryant,

> Apparently no editorial pencil ever
> touched the pages of CYCLE OF THE WERE-
> WOLF. The text was rife with typos.
> Funny--with a $29 book, one expects the
> publisher at least to proofread the
> text. But then on the jacket, the pub-
> lisher apparently doesn´t know the dif-
> ference between "phenomena" and phenom-
> enon." (19)

In addition, the text refers to weapons that do
not exist: a Colt Woodsman .38 and a .45 Magnum.
Such difficulties alter the work, he concludes, by
breaking the illusion of reality. If "part of
Stephen King´s effectiveness is his ability to
suck readers into a recreated every day world,"
these distractions threaten to "break the spell"
(19). Fortunately, with the appearance of the
Signet edition, most of these "niggling little
wrong details" have disappeared; Cycle of the
Werewolf is both accessible and accurate. For the
first time, King´s general readership can enjoy
his one extended treatment of the werewolf.

The Walking Dead . . . and Others

Beyond ghosts, haunted houses, vampires, and
werewolves lies a vast range of additional horrors, limited only by imagination--the writer´s
and the reader´s.
Some of King´s creatures are easily classifi-
able. The amorphous thing in "Crouch End," like
the monstrous possessed and possessing woman in
"Gramma" or the giant rats in "Graveyard Shift"
and other stories, reflects Lovecraft´s Cthulhu
mythos. Character, setting, and imagery in "Nona"
suggest Poe at his graphic best.
Others filter through King´s imagination and
emerge altered from their originals. As closely
related as the creature in "The Raft" may be to
The Blob, it retains King´s unique touch. It is at
once frightening and mysterious. The description
of Deke´s death, as the creature forces his body

through a crack less than an inch wide, is one of
the most graphically realized passages in King's
fiction, creating the visceral response Lovecraft
and others have argued is necessary in effective
horror fiction. At the same time, the play of
colors across and through the creature, the inexplicable power it exerts over Randy, and its
apparent promise of beauty suggesting that it is
ultimately a metaphor for unattainable artistic
expression (at least in the earlier version), elevate the creature from a mindless protoplasmic
entity, as in The Blob, and increase its symbolic
value. If there is a beauty in the creature that
can only be apprehended by risking self and identity, and if experiencing that beauty might itself
be worth death, "The Raft" could almost be read
dually as a tale of dark fantasy and as an allegory for the obsession that can result from art
and creation.

On a more literal level, we find a troll in
"The General," the third segment of Cat's Eye. In
Night Shift, boogeymen hiding in closets reveal
the face beneath rationality and reality; King's
choice of a psychiatrist as the boogeyman's mask
strengthens the symbolic value of that story. In
"The Crate," King re-works a cartoon character,
the Tasmanian devil, while "The Night of the Tiger" insinuates real animals into the texture of
horror. Even the simple act of relaxing and
drinking beer can be fraught with danger, as King
illustrates in "Gray Matter."

Occasionally, King moves into the realms of
gods and demons. "Sometimes They Come Back" encompasses demonology; "Children of the Corn"
blends demon and god in "He Who Walks Behind the
Rows," imagistically a conflation of pagan deity
with Christian ritual and unfairly transformed
into a Hollywood boogeyman in the film version.
"The Lawnmower Man" reaches into classical mythology to resurrect Pan as nature god, while "Mrs.
Todd's Shortcut" avoids almost all of the elements
of horror (except, of course, for the strange
creatures found on her car's bumper) to create an
eerily optimistic tale of Olympus and its occasional and tengential connections with our world.

Yet of all of King's creatures, the most
effective for the contemporary reader might be the
walking dead. Based in part on George A. Romero's

visualization of shambling creatures in <u>Night of the Living Dead</u> (1968) and <u>Dawn of the Dead</u> (1979), King´s version of the walking dead appears briefly in <u>The Shining</u>, to the extent that Wendy´s knife kills Jack yet his body continues to function. Only later do the walking dead become a central motif, with the unfinished "Skybar" (1982) and the derivative "Father´s Day" and "Something to Tide You Over" segments from <u>Creepshow</u> (1982), a collaborative work with Romero based on the old E.C. comics.

All of this is prefatory, however, to King´s definitive (to date, at least) statement on the walking dead: <u>Pet Sematary</u> (1983), completed in May of 1979, withheld for several years, then revised in 1982 prior to publication. King´s original reponse to the manuscript was that it was too dark, too unrelievedly intense for him to feel comfortable with it. The last of King´s novels from Doubleday, <u>Pet Sematary</u> appeared as a means of meeting a contract requirement--what Winter calls "ransom for substantial money, earned by King´s early novels, that had been withheld from him" (<u>Art</u> 131-132).

Even before it was published, the novel stimulated interest and controversy. In part because of the nature of the contract that resulted in its publication, King refused to promote the novel; his question-and-answer session with Douglas Winter at the International Conference on the Fantastic in the Arts (March 1984) was one of the few times that he spoke publicly about the book. His reticence enhanced Doubleday´s publicity hype that the novel was too horrific even for Stephen King, a claim in part dispelled by King´s current work on a screen version in conjunction with George A. Romero.

It seems fitting that <u>Pet Sematary</u> conclude a chapter called "Ghosties and Ghoulies . . ."; it is an omnibus of horror, including not only the reanimated dead but also ghosts, premonitions, dark houses and creaking floors, threatening shadows, things that go bump, and even a "long-legged beastie," if one chooses to so describe the mysterious, almost formless Wendigo that passes Louis Creed in the night.

Even more effectively, it weaves these ele-

85

ments into a narrative firmly based in reality: people, places, and events reflect King's life. Louis Creed works as doctor-in-residence at the University of Maine at Orono, King's alma mater. In a recent letter discussing Rage, King wrote that he originally submitted the novel under his grandfather's name; Guy Pillsbury, he added, was "a great guy and a Jud Crandall prototype if ever there was one" (Letter, 3 August 1985). One of the first critical episodes, the death of the Creed's cat, Winston Churchill, grew out of the death of King's daughter's cat. Three days after burying the cat, the idea for Pet Sematary came to King; recalling an experience with his son Owen running toward a road, King made an imaginative leap:

> . . . on one side of this two-lane high-way was the idea of what if the cat came back, and on the other side of the highway was what if the kid came back --so that when I reached the other side, I had been galvanized by the idea, but not in any melodramatic way. I knew im-mediately that it was a novel. (Winter, Art 130)

It was a novel--but a difficult one for King to write and for his readers to accommodate. A first reading can be misleading; for someone wanting another 'Salem's Lot, The Stand, or Chris-tine, Pet Sematary seems long, drawn-out, and slow, swirling muddily and interminably (it seems) around the figure of Church the cat, then accom-plishing the final horror in only a few pages. A second reading suggests a different structure, however. The novel does move slowly through the early actions, concentrating on the minutiae of reality, as if Louis Creed were desperately trying to retain his hold on what he knows is true, even as he is drawn inexorably into what he can only hope may be. The pacing becomes part of King's structure, emphasizing Creed's unwillingness (and perhaps King's) to confront the horror. When it comes, it proves almost overwhelming; the figure of the child-thing coldly murdering its mother may be too much for even the master of horror to con-template. Michael Stamm writes that the finale of this unusually grim novel seems

> relentlessly horrifying, but somehow in-
> appropriate--as well as less complex and
> frightening than it might have been,
> ghastly though it is. It is as if King
> wanted to get <u>out</u> of the story's awful
> darkness and was less careful than usual
> about how he did so. (36)

One result of this conjunction of elements is
that <u>Pet Sematary</u> repays a second reading . . .
and a third. To do so is not to revel in gratu-
itous blood and death but rather to establish a
distance from the immediate narrative, allowing a
more objective assessment of what King has
achieved. To refer again to Stamm's review, the
novel "<u>is</u> a harrowing story, plumbing depths of
blackness King has never reached--nor, I think,
wanted to reach--before." It attains to a dark
poetry, its landscape "peopled with ancient shadows drifting more and more thickly around the
lives of the storied inhabitants, and the reader
senses the coming of a night [without] end" (36).
In its incessant darkness, <u>Pet Sematary</u> engages disturbing issues, the most apparent being
the nature of death and of our reactions to it.
As a number of readers have noted, it re-works W.
W. Jacob's short story, "The Monkey's Paw." That
story begins, in good Gothic fashion, on a dark
and stormy night, with father and son playing
chess, "the former, who possessed ideas about the
game involving radical changes, putting his king
into such sharp and unnecessary perils that it
even provoked comment from the white-haired old
lady knitting placidly by the fire" (592). This
desire for "radical changes" leads to the climax
of the story: the old man receives a talisman that
will fulfill three wishes. His first (modest
enough) is for two hundred pounds. When the son
is killed in a gruesome accident and the employers
give the old couple two hundred pounds "in consid-
eration of your son's services" (599), the father
realizes the true nature of the talisman and its
accompanying wishes. As Sergeant Major Morris
said, the paw "had a spell put on it by an old
fakir . . . , a very holy man. He wanted to show
that fate ruled people's lives, and that those who

interfered with it did so to their sorrow" (594). Morris, we are told, has had his three wishes; he not only refuses to speak of them but his face blanches at the memory.

In spite of the warnings and the tragic effect the talisman has already had on their lives, the old man wishes for an even more radical change: "I wish my son alive again" (601). Unfortunately, with the short-sightedness of so many characters in so many stories, he fails to modify the wish. Later, hearing repeated knocks on his door and realizing what he has in fact wished for, he "found the monkey's paw, and frantically breathed his third and last wish" (603).

Jacobs does not define the last wish, nor does he describe who (or what) was knocking on the door; the reader's imagination is sufficient to fill in both. What is important, however, is that the story reaffirms the role of death in human lives and closes on a note of acceptance. There has been a tragedy, followed by a disruption of the natural order; but finally there is restoration of that order and a dark, somnolent peace: "The street lamp flickering opposite shone on a quiet and deserted road" (603). At the last moment, Mr. White learned the same lesson that Sergeant Major Morris apparently had.

Louis Creed, however, does not learn. King retains the motif of three "wishes," altering the third almost beyond recognition. Although a doctor and thus familiar with death (as the early episode concerning Victor Pascow illustrates), Louis Creed cannot accept the changes Church's death will bring; like Mr. White, he chooses to base his game of chess on radical change. And like the Whites, he attempts to explain away Church's re-appearance as coincidence; the cat was not actually dead, only stunned. He knows better, as the Whites know better, but embraces self-deception rather than admit a more disturbing truth: that he has disrupted the natural order, invoking the mysterious and evil powers of the Wendigo inherent in the ground of the cemetery.

His second action parallels precisely the Whites' second wish: "I wish my son alive again." In spite of what he knows about Church, in spite of the stories Jud Crandall tells about Timmy Baterman and the Micmac burial ground, in spite of

88

Crandall's explicit warnings and the premonitory
episode of the broken casket in the funeral home--
in spite of all, Creed, like White, is seduced by
the possibility of reversing death. His "wish" is
not as easy or clean as White's; King details
Creed's visit to the cemetery, his painful and
fatiguing hike to the Micmac grounds, his desper-
ate vigil waiting for whatever was to come, and
his falling asleep and the terrible consequences
of that lapse. As in "The Monkey's Paw" the core
of the narrative, this second "wish" underscores
Louis Creed's unwillingness to accept death and
his abrogation of everything that he, as a physician, knows and represents.

With the third "wish," Creed confirms his insanity. White struggled desperately to find the
monkey's paw in the darkness, even as he heard his
wife's pleas that he help her unlock the door and
let their son into the house. In the end, at the
last moment, White chose to restore order by
retracting the radical change he had made in the
game.

Creed does not. Instead, he descends further
into darkness, paradoxically symbolized by his
hair turning white as Nadine Cross's hair turned
white when she embraced darkness in the person of
the Walkin Dude in The Stand. Instead of relin-
quishing the dead to death, he compounds his
error, taking Rachel's body to the Micmac burying
grounds and perversely insisting on his third
"wish." Later, covering the threateningly symbolic queen of spades with his hand, he listens as
his wife approaches, her voice "grating, full of
dirt" (374). Pet Sematary has reached its nearly
unbearable conclusion.

"The Monkey's Paw" horrifies by implication.
Jacobs shows nothing, specifies nothing; readers
must fill the interstices between words and by
doing so create the horror themselves. Pet Sematary, on the other hand, works through explicit
representation. Again and again we see the disastrous results of altering fate: pets returning
from the children's cemetery changed in subtle
ways; a bull so vicious that it must be destroyed;
Church's stiffness and lack of grace (an ironically ambiguous word in this context), and his
depredations against birds, nauseatingly detailed
in full color; the horror of Timmy Baterman and

the tragic events required to restore the irrevocability of death.

In _Pet Sematary_, King emphasizes the failure of two social structures designed to accommodate (or at least offset) our fear of death. As a physician, Louis Creed knows that death can sometimes be delayed but never vanquished; living organisms die. Victor Pascow's accident underscores Creed's inability to accept death. At first, as the dying man whispers "In the Pet Sematary," Creed tries to rationalize it away. Like White in "The Monkey's Paw," he speaks of coincidence, of "auditory hallucination" or a chance blending of phonemes.

Yet when Pascow fixes him with a grin like "the large grin of a dead carp" and speaks his cryptically premonitory words--"It's not the real cemetery" and "The soil of a man's heart is stonier, Louis . . . A man grows what he can . . . and tends it"--Louis's physician's rationalism falters. He cannot account for the statements or for the fact that Pascow knows his name; nor can he accept the violence of Pascow's death.

Although Pascow's appearance later as a ghost is consistent with King's narrative purposes and provides a sudden intrusion of the irrational into the novel to presage more devastating intrusions, it seems equally designed as a symbolic statement of Louis Creed's inability to accept death. In a sense, Creed conjures the boy's shade by his obsessive reaction to death. In spite of his attempts to explain his reactions--and the leaves and dirt on his sheets the next morning--part of Louis Creed believes that death is not the end. He rejects the medical view of death as natural and inevitable.

If _Pet Sematary_ anatomizes the medical mind, it also explores the religious. King notes that his characters are not strongly religious. Louis Creed, he says, "was a man with no deep religious training, no bent toward the superstitious or the occult" (58-59); Rachel denies her childhood religious training.

More tantalizingly, King gives his characters names that argue for the failure of religion in contemporary society. Victor Pascow dies and by doing so shows Louis Creed what dying is like. _Pascow_ is startlingly similar to _Paschal_ (of or related to either Easter or Passover); the differ-

ence between the two words is almost, as Louis
Creed might argue, a chance divergence of phonemes.

On the basis of one resemblance in sound, of
course, it seems reckless to construct a literary
interpretation, particularly in light of King's
comment that his character's names rarely imply
conscious symbolism. In this instance, however,
there is additional justification. Pascow's presence in the novel serves only one purpose: to
initiate Louis Creed's confrontation with death.
Pascow dies a horrible, lingering, and painful
death. By doing so he becomes one of King's recurring sacrificial children, dying in order that
the main character might more fully understand
life and death; he is almost literally, as his
name suggests figuratively, a sacrificial lamb.
There is, however, no resurrection for Victor
Pascow except as a ghost; his first name is as
ironic as his last is symbolic.

Pascow's death is only the first in a series
connected to a theological undercurrent. The
second is the death of Winston Churchill, the cat.
In spite of the cat's name, and in contradiction
to King's occasional introduction of political motifs in his narratives, the cat suggests religion
rather than politics. With few exceptions, the
cat is simply called "Church." The death of
Church (i.e., the church) beneath the wheels of a
huge truck that represents industrialized, technological society is too overt a motif to ignore,
even though the novel does not develop an explicit
theological message; King's intent emerges subtly,
through the shadows as it were. Church's death
does not help Louis Creed adapt to death. Instead, it provides another springboard for his
descent into darkness and horror. "Church"
becomes ironic as the cat returns, graceless and
fallen, to stand as a constant reminder of Louis
Creed's own moment of weakness.

The final link is a double one. Gage Creed
and Rachel Creed both die, are buried in the Micmac burying gound, and return . . . changed.
Their surname, Creed, insists upon a theological
interpretation; not only is the church as institu-
tion unable to give meaning to contemporary life
(Louis is a "lapsed" Methodist, Rachel a "lapsed"
Jew), but belief itself dies. Gage's death paral-

lels Church's beneath the wheels of a truck; he is
three days in the darkness of death, then resur-
rected into deeper darkness. To make a horrible
pun (but one appropriate to Pet Sematary), Louis
Creed is the father, Gage Creed the son, and Victor Pascow the unholy ghost, all circling the dead
and mechanical Church. Rachel, like Melville's
ship in Moby Dick a type for mourning Israel after
the sacrifice of the infants, returns to seek her
lost child; by doing so, yet another "creed" is
lost. Only one remains: Eileen is safe at her
grandparents', but given Rachel's experiences in
that home, even that refuge seems superficial and
threatening.

All of this may seem to place an inordinate
burden of symbolism and analogy on the novel, but
King invites the burden. Pet Sematary is, as Gary
Goshgarian argues, inbued with questions of moral
responsibility. By introducing Louis Creed's scientific rationalism and his rejection of faith; by
re-creating the trauma of Rachel's childhood and
her abnormal fear of death removed from the support of religion; and by giving his characters
names that echo underlying moral questions, King
insists that Pet Sematary be read as more than
just a ghost story or an excursion into the horror
landscape of the walking dead.

Goshgarian's conclusion merits repeating
since it sums up the dark attraction of Pet Sematary:

> Yes, his vampires, demons and zom-
> bies are deliciously horrible--but it is
> between those familiar monsters that
> King shows his true art--an art that in-
> vites us to contemplate our own mortal-
> ity. King does not believe in ghouls,
> vampires and zombies. But he does be-
> lieve in real-life demons like war, vio-
> lence, disease and death and, perhaps
> the most frightening thing in the known
> universe: the human mind. (8)

The inexorable movement of Pet Sematary gives it a
deliberation unusual for King, yet consonant with
the novel's tone. As Edward Bryant says:

> Even though Pet Sematary flinches at the

end, that does not deny the innate power
of the balance of the novel. Incom-
pletely realized as it is, I still think
the book supports my view of the writer.
It´s stretching, pushing things to the
limit, that causes the author to grow.
It is only through experiments such as
Pet Sematary, painful and difficult as
they may be, that Stephen King will
cross that hazy but undeniable line between good and great. (19)

When King approaches greatness, as he does in "The
Reach," for example, it is because he penetrates
beneath surface distinctions such as "horror," or
"fantasy," or "mainstream" to touch his readers at
the core.

In Pet Sematary, he approaches that intensity.

During a session at the International Conference on the Fantastic, King was asked why he let
so many children die in his novels, especially Tad
Trenton in Cujo and Gage Creed in Pet Sematary.
His answer: in the real world, children die. They
die of cancer; they get hit by trucks. And that
is the real horror.

Later, in an interview with David Sherman, he
repeated that stance:

There´s a little girl in Pet Sematary
who lives. Nobody else lives. And
there´s no rhyme or reason for it.
There´d be more justification in that
story--in the sense of a final tying up
of loose ends--if she died, too. But
that isn´t the way life is. (16)

93

Chapter VI

ONE IN EVERY GARAGE: THE MACHINE AMOK

<u>Christine</u>

In late September 1985, as King was directing
<u>Maximum Overdrive</u>, one of the sequences to be shot
involved a runaway lawnmower. According to King's
description, the machine

> really <u>did</u> get away. It struck the
> wedges under the camera, showering us
> all with splinters. Several people were
> cut, I was completely untouched, and Ar-
> mando [Nanuzzi, the film's cinematog-
> rapher] sustained an injury that's put
> him in the Duke Eye Care clinic. We re-
> sume next Wednesday. I'm still shaken.
> <u>All</u> the machines on this project really
> seem malevolent. (Letter, 3 August 1985)

It may seem appropriate, in a perversely symbolic
sense, that a lawnmower "attack" King and his
crew, since he has frequently represented machines
as sentient, malevolent, and violent.

In several stories, King abandons the possibilities of traditional horror--ghosts, vampires,
werewolves, and other creatures of myth and leg-
end--to concentrate on a variant more compatible
with and inherent in twentieth-century technology.
We orient ourselves around machines; we trust
machines and depend upon them, occasionally excor-
iating them but finally recognizing their importance in our lives.

Even so, the suspicion remains, nagging at
our consciousness, that somehow "they" are out to
get us. Cars that won't start, electrical gadgets
that choose the most inopportune moment to expire
in a spray of sparks and black smoke, typewriters

94

and computers that behave perfectly until the crucial moment halfway through a research paper (or a
book of criticism)--these and similar situations
prove rich ground for the imagination.

For most of us, such episodes merely frus-
trate; for the writers of horror fiction, they may
stimulate speculation and questioning. Working
from a common, everyday object, King twists our
perceptions of that object by endowing the thing
with life, sentience, mobility, or just a healthy
dash of horror. The results include the runaway
ironing machine of "The Mangler"; the voracious
and deadly mower in "The Lawnmower Man"; rebellious automobiles determined to supplant humanity
as masters in "Trucks"; a derelict vehicle that
makes its own revenge in "Uncle Otto´s Truck";
children´s toys that become instruments of death
and (again) revenge in "Battleground"; another
child´s toy that delights in mayhem for the sake
of mayhem in "The Monkey"; and finally a machine
that, unlike the others, alters reality to restore
fairness and justice in the eminently unfair world
of "Word Processor of the Gods."

And, of course, there is Christine.

King´s fascination with the deadly effects of
"machines" (if we can use the word rather loosely
for a moment) developed early in his career. "The
Star Invaders" depends upon machines: the torture
room of the Invaders and Jed Pierce´s ray-cannon
are essential to the plot but depend upon external
agents. In "The Glass Floor," an artifact, the
mirrored floor, similarly functions passively; human responses rather than the artifact itself
generate the specific horror. In "The Reaper´s
Image," another mirror initiates the action but
again as a vehicle for an inexplicably deeper
active principle. Later, in "The Blue Air Compressor," King links a machine more tightly to an
image of horror; again, however, human manipulation initiates the action. Although these "machines" may be destructive, they are neither
self-motile nor inherently sentient. The horror
in those stories depends upon human (or alien but
organic) agency.

Gradually, however, King introduced a variant
in his stories. The machines move. They rip
themselves from the concrete floors of the Blue
Ribbon Laundry and rumble down city streets in

search of victims. They trap humans inside a truck stop and force one-time masters to serve them as slaves. They become agents of revenge, vehicles (pun intended) for transporting ordinary characters across the boundaries into horror and dark fantasy. They epitomize our deepest fears and most disturbing nightmares.

In "The Monkey," for example, King masterfully transforms a simple child's toy into an image of terror, capitalizing on a childhood fear and then transferring it, fully developed and justified by the evidence of Hal Shelburn's senses, into an adult. The only other character who understands the threat the monkey poses is his younger and more innocently child-like son, Petey. The older boy, Dennis, has begun to enter the adult world; he is twelve, and the fact that he reacts to the monkey with a respectful "Hey, neat" is critical since, as King points out, "It was a tone Hal rarely got from the boy anymore himself" (SC 141). Later, in an emotional confrontation with Dennis (148-149), Shelburn recognizes the gap age has created between himself and his older son. As with so many of King's characters, Shelburn can only watch as his family fragments.

With Petey, however, he can re-create, face, and finally lay to rest lingering childhood fears, since Petey is young enough to believe in such things . . . and Shelburne is old enough again, to paraphrase C. S. Lewis's prefatory letter to The Lion, The Witch, and The Wardrobe, to accept an intrusion of the fantastic into his life. Together, father and son bridge the years as they fight against the threat of the toy monkey.

"The Monkey" is a fascinating excursion into childhood horror made adult (see SW 137-138), with well-rounded characters and a complex plot requiring multiple flashbacks that gradually reveal the horror of the childhood toy. As with so many of King's narratives, it describes an external evil imposing itself on an innocent--a toy that, no matter how many times it is thrown away, manages to come back . . . and kill.

An even more interesting element, however, is an implicit connection in the final pages between the monkey and King's ultimate monster-machine, Christine. As Shelburn throws the bag containing the toy overboard, he looks into the water:

> there was Amos Culligan´s Studebaker,
> and Hal´s mother was behind its slimy
> wheel, a grinning skeleton with a lake
> bass staring coldly from one fleshless
> eye socket. Uncle Will and Aunt Ida
> lolled beside her, and Aunt Ida´s gray
> hair trailed upward as the bag fell
> . . . .
> Hal slammed the oars back into the
> water, scraping blood from his knuckles
> (and ah God the back of Amos Culligan´s
> Studebaker had been fill of dead chil-
> dren! Charlie Silverman . . . Johnny
> McCabe . . .), and began to bring the
> boat about. (170)

The image prefigures Christine, a haunted machine
similarly filled with unnerving passengers. The
conclusion of "The Monkey," with its calmly factu-
al newspaper article and its suggestion that the
monkey has not relinquished its power to destroy,
equally foreshadows the final pages of Christine.
King´s choice of name for the by-line--"Betsy Mor-
iarity"--conflates innocence with experience; a
childlike, almost pastoral sense blends with a
hint of Conan Doyle´s murderer in the Sherlock
Holmes tales. Although to push the resemblance any
further would injure the story, even a detail as
apparently minor as this journalist´s name underscores the ambivalence King´s characters (and
perhaps King himself) feel toward the toy monkey
and its final destruction, an emotion parallelled
and amplified in Christine. In King´s universe,
evil can only rarely be destroyed; more often it
merely lies in wait for another try.

Of King´s major works, Christine (1983) lends
itself most readily to a symbolic interpretation.
Like Roadwork, which was written during roughly
the time frame of the novel (August 1972 to
January 1974), Christine seems a product of its
time. It is, with the earlier book, a distinctly
post-energy-crisis novel harkening back to a less
restricted relationship between Americans and
their automobile; it is, in a phrase, about the
end of a love affair.
The text itself virtually demands such a symbolic reading. The first lines define the complex

of loyalties to be tested through the novel:

> This is the story of a lover's tri-
> angle, I suppose you'd say--Arnie Cun-
> ningham, Leigh Cabot, and, of course,
> Christine. But I want you to understand
> that Christine was there first. She was
> Arnie's first love . . . . (1)

At first, nothing seems amiss in this description
. . . until one discovers that Christine is a 1958
Plymouth Fury. At that point, King moves beyond
reality and into a world of hauntings and malevolent machinery. Yet underlying the irrationali-
ties and impossibilities suddenly made enforcedly
rational and possible is the fact of a changing
America: an economy shifting in part away from
dependence upon the automobile and increasingly
obsessed with small, fuel-efficient cars. Next to
the Toyotas or Volkswagens of 1983, Christine
seems a monster in more ways than one.

Coupled to this overt reading is a second,
amplifying the first and making possible the
tragedy of Christine. The America of the late
seventies perceived itself as mature. It had,
after all, successfully negotiated the turmoil of
the sixties; it had recently passed its two
hundredth anniversary, with sufficient concommi-
tant hoopla to convince itself that it had fully
come of age; and it had begun looking back on the
1950s as a time of adolescence preparatory to
entry into adulthood.

Coming of age forms a critical motif in
Christine. Built in 1958, Christine is in her
twenty-first year, approaching her majority, as it
were. Arnie Cunningham, Dennis Guilder, and Leigh
Cabot are seniors in high school. The question of
Arnie's finally making his own decisions, including his choice of which college to attend or even
whether to attend college at all, creates a
continuing theme in the novel, parallelling his
increasing obsession with and finally possession
by Christine. At bottom is the question of his
age: is he near enough adult to be responsible for
his own decisions? Arnie says he is and asserts
his new independence by impulsively buying Christine; Regina Cunningham insists that he is not and
risks alienating her only son by refusing to

compromise until it is too late.

As a result, characters and names reflect a historical era closely associated with transition in American culture and society. Having Christine a 1958 model firmly ties the novel to the late fifties, as do King´s references to rock songs from the same period, allusions so important that he included them in spite of the healthy fee required for permissions: $15,000, to be paid by King, Viking, and NAL ("King New Book"). The car symbolizes adolescence, obsessive and possessive in her absorption of Arnie´s developing personality, paralleling society´s transition from the adolescent fifties to the adult eighties.

Arnie Cunningham´s name also connects King´s novel of contemporary adolescence with the archetypal representation of television adolescence, Happy Days. "Cunningham" is, of course, the surname of the central family in that long-running paean to the fifties; "Richie," the diminutive for "Richard"; and "Arnold´s," the central hang-out. Christine thus includes a double allusion to Richie Cunningham and Happy Days in Arnold Richard Cunningham (353). Arnie is television´s Richie gone bad, with Dennis Guilder as the more positive role model: solid, intelligent, responsible, devoted to his family but nonetheless capable of independent thought and action. To carry the parallels even further, Buddy Repperton suggests the kind of character Arthur "Fonzie" Fonzarelli was originally intended to represent, before he mellowed into a contemporary cult figure.

Christine explores the rites associated with coming of age in our society--or perhaps better said, the lack of rites. Arnie is initially helpless to assert his increasingly adult identity. Only with the arrival of Christine does he find an external object of sufficient importance to challenge Regina´s authority. Like characters in Rage, The Long Walk, Carrie, Firestarter, or The Talisman, Arnie must accept and understand change while simultaneously becoming aware of the dangers inherent in growing up.

More importantly, he begins to define his changing relationship with his parents. Arnie exemplifies the fragmentation and isolation within the family unit typical in King´s fictions when, early in the novel, he asks if Dennis has realized

99

that "parents are nothing but overgrown kids until
their children drag them into adulthood? Usually
kicking and screaming?" (26). Later, the accusa-
tion and the implicit separation of parent and
child become more threatening: "I think that part
of being a parent is trying to kill your kids,"
Arnie asserts. "Because as soon as you have a
kid, you know for sure that you're going to die.
When you have a kid, you see your own gravestone"
(26, 27). As blunt as Arnie's comment is, King
provides additional support for it much later when
Dennis asks George LeBay if Roland LeBay had in
fact "offered his daughter up as some kind of a
human sacrifice." The best response George LeBay
can provide is a long silence and a hesitant, "Not
in any conscious way, no" (453).

Part of Arnie's frustration stems from the
image his parents present and consequently from
the threat that he may become like them, yet
neither fully himself nor fully them; throughout,
he sees himself as sacrificed to their perceptions
of what he should be. He insists that he be al-
lowed to follow his own path; unfortunately, in
spite of his protestations, he fails the test.

Nor is Arnie alone. Dennis Guilder is in
some ways as central a character as Arnie. He
narrates two thirds of the novel, an unusual
occurrence in King, since only Rage (also an
examination of adolescent adjustment to on-coming
adulthood) provides that kind of subjectivity.
Later, when Dennis is in the hospital and incapable of narrating events, King simply shifts to
third person without explanation or apology,
moving back to Dennis for the final chapters.
Dennis has his own adjustments to make. He sees
his years-long influence over Arnie diminish--as
rightly it should--but for the wrong reasons. He
sees Arnie first win then abandon Leigh Cabot.
And he sees what Christine is and how she changes
Arnie. Knowing what he does, Dennis must likewise
choose between a child's response and an adult's.
He can either tell what he knows and depend upon
the adults (in this case his substantially more
responsive parents) to rectify matters, or take
action himself and by doing so thrust himself into
a world of self-sufficiency.

Wisely, he chooses the latter. His parents
are unusually understanding, questioning as long

100

as they sense that they are helping, backing off
when it becomes clear that Dennis must make
serious decisions, trusting him to take the right
action. Their trust saves their lives, just as
Michael Cunningham's failure to heed Dennis'
warnings about Christine eventually leads to his
death.

In _Christine_, children must act as adults.
As they do so, they shed light both on themselves
and on what they may become. If there is a trian-
gle in _Christine_ it might as justifiably be
defined as Arnie, Christine, and Dennis. Standing
on each side of the monstrous machine, Arnie and
Dennis illustrate opposing responses to the irrational, the inexplicable, the fantastic, and the
horrific. Dennis, of course, comes off best; that
he narrates the story from the vantage of hind-
sight allows him, however unconsciously, to recast
events in his own favor. In this case, the
first-person voice throws doubt on the narrator
himself. Regardless of this complication, however, Dennis does defeat Christine, if only
temporarily; Arnie succumbs, becomes entrapped by
the evil presence of the dead Roland LeBay, and
only emerges at the end long enough to destroy his
possessor even as he kills himself.

Christine and the ghostly presence of Roland
LeBay symbolize externally Arnie's internal
changes as he struggles for individuality and
freedom. A child becoming involved in things beyond his understanding or control, Arnie can also
function symbolically in the novel. Christine or
LeBay provide explicit pressures and temptations,
with Will Darnell acting as an additional force
for evil.

On one level, such a reading is possible.
And even on that restricted a level, _Christine_ is
an intriguing and empathetic portrait of failure
and false choice.

There is, of course, only one problem with
stopping at that point.

Christine _is_ haunted.

Again and again in the novel, characters shut
their eyes to the irrational, refusing to accept
it within their well-ordered, carefully defined
perceptions of reality. As late as chapter 45,
Dennis still must fight with that simple fact:
there is something beyond reason happening to him,

to Arnie, and to Leigh. It takes him a long time
to accept the unacceptable. After a difficult
night assessing evidence and events, he says that
his mind "had already begun to heal itself with
unreality. My problem was that I could simply no
longer afford to listen to that lulling song. The
line was blurred for good" (439).

That blurred line is crucial in Christine.
It is not enough to talk of the novel as an adolescent rite of passage, as an anatomy of teen-
agers growing up and away from parents, or even,
as King has, as a discussion of sex substitutes
and sublimation. It is that, of course, but more.

From the beginning, King makes it clear that
there is something supernatural involved. Arnie's
choices are not entirely his own, increasingly so
as the novel progresses and Christine's hold intensifies. The fundamental problem is that, as
Darnell realizes, "most people would accept anything if they saw it happen right before their
very eyes. In a very real sense there was no supernatural, no abnormal: what happened, happened,
and that was the end" (316).

Reference after reference, however, makes it
clear that Arnie, Dennis, Leigh, and those surrounding them are in the midst of something evil,
frightening, and inexplicable. At first, King
merely suggests the supernatural; Leigh worries
about Arnie, thinking that Christine seems almost
like a vampire (290). Later, King drops all pre-
tense of simile--Dennis sees the ghost of LeBay in
the car.

As if to insure the persistence of danger,
King not only connects Christine with the ghosts
and ghoulies of The Shining and the vampires of
'Salem's Lot, but neatly suggests that even had
Arnie capitulated and accepted his mother's dicta
concerning Christine, he would not necessarily
have been safe; after all, both Regina and Michael
teach at the University in Horlicks, well known to
King's readers as the site of "The Crate" and "The
Raft."

Connections between "The Raft" and Christine
multiply upon close examination. Young people,
barely adults, are isolated and threatened by an
unexplainable entity that seems intent upon ab-
sorbing them--in one literally, in the other figuratively. In each, sexuality intrudes as a

threatening principle. In "The Raft," Randy and
LaVerne make love; the action leads to her death.
In Christine, Dennis and Leigh form a similar
attachment which, while not expressed physically,
nonetheless places both in jeopardy from Christine. Earlier, of course, Leigh's growing love
for Arnie similarly brought events to a crisis as
she nearly choked to death in Christine. In each
instance, sexuality becomes an image of maturity,
intruding complication and danger.

There are also differences between the novel
and the story, of course. "The Raft" asserts a
shapeless creature; Christine merges the creature
with the most pervasive machine in our society.
"The Raft" sets the four students physically
apart from others; in Christine, the isolation is
more psychological as each character discovers
things about Christine and the dead LeBay that
cannot be talked about. And finally, the conclusions move in quite different directions. In
spite of King's additions to the Skeleton Crew
version of the story, shifting its emphasis more
stridently toward Randy's fear of and final rejection of maturity and the adult world, "The Raft,"
even in its original form, is highly pessimistic.
There is no relief, no hope except that the mysterious play of color on the creature can at least
remove the pain. Christine ends more optimistically. For the moment at least, the threat is
removed. Sexuality ceases to bring danger; Dennis
and Leigh consummate their relationship, then
gradually grow apart to establish new lives as
adults. In spite of the fear that Christine is on
the move again, the novel could be said to have a
positive ending. Even Arnie ultimately succeeds
(or so Dennis hopes), surfacing long enough to
destroy LeBay.

Indeed, the novel closes on an awkward note.
In spite of an insistence on the surface techniques and characteristics of horror, Dennis and
Leigh subordinate the horror and terror inspired
by ghosts and malevolent machines to a deeper
emotion: sorrow. After his nightmare ride in
Christine, as the landscape itself shifts and
blurs between 1978 and 1958, Dennis says
good-night to Arnie: "I shut the door," he says.
"My horror had changed to a deep and terrible
sorrow--it was as if [Arnie] had been buried.

Buried alive" (437). The sense increases later as, just before the final confrontation in Darnell's garage, Dennis challenges the LeBay-thing within Arnie: "There was no Arnie in it now. No Arnie at all. My friend was gone. I felt a dark sorrow that was deeper than tears or fear . . ." (480). At the end, there is neither the quiet optimism of The Stand or the abysmal darkness of Pet Sematary; there is only a deep sense of loss that nearly overpowers the possibility of a threat renewed. Lives change; Dennis and Leigh emerge fully as adults. The children they were--the child that Arnie was--are lost forever.

Christine has been criticized as heavily as any of King's novels. It is too long, many reviewers argued, almost submerging the narrative in King's gush of unnecessary words. The language is more consistently harsh than in other novels, in part because of the characters' ages; obscenity seems one of the few outlets our society provides for youth trying to emulate what they consider adults to be. Still, as justifiable as it might be in the context of plot, character, and theme, the language does invite criticism.

In addition, the self-absorption with rock 'n' roll throughout also draws from the main story. Again, the allusions function on one level as thematic connectors, linking present time with King's (and his readers') past. Occasionally, however, that thematic function seems inadequate to support the weight of intrusion and allusion King insists upon.

And finally, Christine undergoes a narrative shift. King has indicated that he originally intended that the novel be told from Dennis' point of view throughout. Only when Dennis suddenly wakes up in the hospital did it become clear that something had to change. The result is an unevenness of texture unusual in King's novels, a shifting of the reader's peceptions that threatens the continuity of narrative and of empathy. Coupled with the ambiguous nature of the narrator, a young man of twenty-two looking back at a critical point in his life, the narrative shift creates an odd disruption.

In spite of all of this, however, reading Christine makes critical comments seem ephemeral. My first contact with the book resulted in a marathon session lasting until well after midnight. The book entranced me, the characters interested me, even the supernatural elements came to seem inevitable in the context of King's fictional world.

If Christine represents one extreme of King's use of machine-monsters, the computer in "Word Processor of the Gods" (1983; SC 1985) represents the other. Published the same year as Christine, the story is much closer to "The Reach" (1981: SC 1985), more optimistic and upbeat than horrifying. Where Christine, the mangler, Uncle Otto's truck, and assorted other maleficent devices disrupt order with chaos, the word processor restores order to the chaos of Richard Nordhoff's life, deleting his monstrous wife and son, inserting his true love (stolen by his brother Roger, a vicious good-for-nothing) and the nephew who should have been Richard's son. Another variant on the three-wishes motif common in fairy tales and explored in Pet Sematary, "Word Processor of the Gods" does much to restore a sense of harmony and balance between humanity and the machines we have created (See SW 147-148).

Chapter VII

EXPLORING TANGENTIAL WORLDS

The Stand, The Dark Tower,
The Eyes of the Dragon, The Talisman

　　While King is best known as a writer of horror fiction, he has also worked in other genres,
including science fiction. Several critics, in
fact, have argued that novels such as Cujo, The
Dead Zone, and Firestarter belong more to science
fiction than to horror. Depending upon the definitions one uses, such an assertion in part rings
true.
　　Even within science fiction, however, King
includes his own twists, often nearly overpowering
the science fictional plots, settings, or characters with touches of the fantastic. In "Beachworld," a seemingly straightforward space adventure transforms into something quite different as
the sand planet is gradually revealed to be a sentient creature as amorphous and unexplainable as
the black blob in "The Raft."
　　King is not alone in this attitude toward the
two genres, of course. Film versions of science
fiction novels frequently emphasize the horrific,
blurring the distinctions between the two; what
Mary Shelley intended as a discussion of responsibility and morality in Frankenstein, for example,
degenerated first into an image of horror and finally into self-parody. As Brian Aldiss says in
Billion Year Spree:

　　　　The cinema has helped enormously to dis-
　　　　seminate the myth while destroying its
　　　　significance . . . . There were short
　　　　silent versions, but the monster began
　　　　his true movie career in 1931, with
　　　　James Whale's Universal picture Franken-
　　　　stein, in which Boris Karloff played the
　　　　monster. The dials in the castle labor-

106

> atory have hardly stopped flickering
> since. The monster has spawned Sons,
> Daughters, Ghosts, and Houses; has taken
> on Brides and created Woman; has per-
> force shacked up with Dracula and Wolf
> Man; has enjoyed Evil, Horror, and
> Revenge, and has even had the Curse: on
> one occasion it met Abbott and Costello.
> (23n)

King's expriences with film show a similar movement. What was originally at least partially
grounded in scientific explanation becomes a show-
case for visual horror, most explicitly in the
film versions of Cujo, which discounts almost entirely the references to a revenant Frank Dodd, or
of Firestarter, with its concentration of images
of destruction and fiery death.

This tendency to tinge science fiction with
horror extends beyond film re-creations of King's
fiction and into his prose itself. What may be
King's most complete attempt at science fiction,
"The Jaunt" (1981, SC 1985; see SW 141-142), is
ostensibly based on the development of almost in-
stantaneous transport between Earth and Mars.
Gradually, however, the tale shifts into subjectivity and insanity, with its final images falling
within the traditions of horror.

The technique is certainly not original with
King, of course. In March 1939, Robert Bloch, one
of the most important influences on King's fiction
(Grant, "Jugular" 21), published "The Strange
Flight of Richard Clayton" in Amazing. The story
recounts Clayton's experiences in a subjective
time-distortion. He survives what he believes a
years-long flight to Mars, coupled with a total
loss of his time-sense and aggravated by hallucin-
ations:

> Ghosts howled, in the dark depths of
> space. Visions of monsters and dreams
> of torment came, and Clayton repulsed
> them all. Every hour or day or year--he
> no longer knew which--Clayton managed to
> stagger to the mirror. And always it
> showed that he was aging rapidly. His
> snow-white hair and wrinkled countenance
> hinted at incredible senility. But

Clayton lived. He was to old to think
any longer, and too weary. He merely
lived in the droning of the ship. (72)

Finally returning to earth, he stumbles from the
capsule into the arms of his assistant . . . who
does not recognize the aged figure.
And then the truth. Clayton manages to ask,
"How long was I in the Future?":

Jerry Chase´s face was grave as he
stared again at the old man and answered, softly.
"Just one week." (73)

The connections between "The Strange Flight
of Richard Clayton" and "The Jaunt" are obvious;
the differences between them are equally obvious.
Bloch explains the time distortion. Clayton had
broken his chronometer; because of a malfunction,
the ship had never taken off, yet the crew could
not approach it for a week. The "droning of the
ship" had merely been the vibrations of its en-
gines. And throughout, Bloch re-creates (as best
he can in a short story, using the conventions of
time and language) Clayton´s subjective experiences. The reader is startled by the surprise
ending, but not specifically horrified.
King, on the other hand, refuses to explain.
He takes his characters only as far as the moment
they enter the subjectivity of the Jaunt, then
resumes his narrative as they emerge on the other
side. If they jaunt in an unconscious state, they
arrive safely; but if they are conscious . . . :

How long in there, in terms of years?
0.000000000067 seconds for the body to
Jaunt, but how long for the unparticu-
lated consciousness? A hundred years? A
thousand? A million? A billion? And how
long with your thoughts in an endless
field of white? And then, when a billion eternities have passed, the crash-
ing return of light and form and body.
Who wouldn´t go insane? (SC 223)

Bloch defines and describes; the result is primarily science fiction. King implies, leaving the

108

reader to imagine what happens; the result is primarily horror.

This is not to say that King cannot write science fiction. Both The Long Walk (1979) and The Running Man (1982) are, strictly speaking, science fiction: they take place in a future America, they depend upon new technologies for the narrative to succeed, and they examine how those technologies change the lives of individuals (see SK/RB 46-69, 92-114). Even there, however, images of horror rest just beneath the surface.

In works such as "The Mist" and "Crouch End," King approaches the boundaries between dark fantasy and science fiction from the opposite direction. In each, the thrust of the story is overtly horror: creatures emerge from the darkness to terrify and destroy. Also in each, however, King provides a marginal explanation. Beyond the universe of the story exist other universes; in "The Mist," scientists at the Arrowhead Project may have punctured the barriers between this universe and others, allowing unnamed and unnameable monsters to spill through. In "Crouch End," the monster, while amorphous and ill-defined, nonetheless belongs to the eldritch worlds of Lovecraftian Great Old Ones. A temporary opening between the two universes allows characters from ours to become lost within alien time and space.

The Stand

Perhaps the most intriguing explorations of alternatives, of worlds tangential to our own, occur in might be called the "Dark Man" narratives: The Stand (1978), The Dark Tower: The Gunslinger (1982), The Eyes of the Dragon (1984), and The Talisman (1984; with Peter Straub). While they are not all explicitly connected by a repeating character as The Stand and The Eyes of the Dragon are, they do explore connections between our world and others.

In terms of genre, The Stand is problematical, since it lacks the monsters and creatures of traditional horror, except for Randall Flagg's occasional shape-shifting. It begins within a science-fictional framework, detailing with the care and precision of hard science fiction the consequences of an escaped super-flu virus; yet

109

just as the characters begin to adjust to the new
world technology has forced upon them, they must
confront something essentially fantastic--their
dreams of Mother Abagail and the Dark Man. Again
and again, King shifts between dark fantasy and
science fiction as the novel turns from the flu to
Randall Flagg (see Collings, "The Stand"). At the
same time, its length and scope link it with the
epic quest, as Ben Indick argued recently in
"Stephen King as Epic Writer" as he points out a
number of thematic and topical resemblances to
Tolkien's The Lord of the Rings.

   In a 1981 interview with King for Twilight
Zone Magazine, Charles L. Grant asked about possible mystical overtones in The Stand, whether the
novel might not be a "Christian allegory," compli-
cating the question of genre even further. King
answered that

>The Stand starts with a plague that
>wipes out most of the world's popula-
>tion, and it develops into a titanic
>struggle that Christianity figures in.
>But it's not about God, like some of the
>reviews claimed. Stuart Redman isn't
>Christ, and the Dark Man isn't the Dev-
>il. . . . The important thing is that we
>are dealing with two elemental forces
>--White and Black--and I really do be-
>lieve in the White force. Children are
>part of that force, which is why I write
>about them the way I do. There are a
>lot of horror writers who deal with this
>struggle, but they tend to concentrate
>on the Black. But the other force is
>there, too; it's just a lot tougher to
>deal with. Look at Tolkien and The Lord
>of the Rings; he's much better at
>evoking the horror and the dread of Mor-
>dor and the Dark Lord than he is at
>doing Gandalf. (23)

Besides the reference to Tolkien, the passage is
important for its definition of what King attempted in the novel. Indick notes that The Stand is
"disconcerting" since it abruptly shifts "from the
initial horror, hopelessness and death, into adventure and hope" ("Epic" 57); that shift signals

King's transition from the almost mandatory pessimism of a science-fictional view of contemporary technology and morality into the cautious optimism of the epic quest. The characters themselves are aware of a subtle alteration in their world, beyond the overt, extreme changes engendered by the superflu. Frannie Goldsmith speculates on one possibility:

> I don't know what to think, except I don't like any of the things that have been happening. Visionary dreams. An old woman who's the voice of God for a while and then walks off into the wilderness. Now a little boy who seems to be a telepath. It's like life in a fairy tale. Sometimes I think the superflu left us alive but drove us all mad. (565)

Rationality versus irrationality, sanity versus madness, a scientific world-view versus overt fantasy--The Stand works through each of these oppositions, testing characters and their assumptions about reality.

That ambivalence lies at the center of The Stand, highlighting its position as a transitional work. For the first time, King allows his novel to transcend reality without depending upon either traditional horror motifs or upon scientific explanations. What little we discover about the superflu explains the deaths of 99.6% of the human population and consequently is important in creating verisimilitude during the early chapters of the novel. Later, however, as King moves from the initial objectivity into the subjectivity of dreams, visions, and the irrational, he refuses to explain. Randall Flagg appears. King suggests that Flagg's personality has taken over someone's body, but insists that Flagg is himself paranormal. He is likened to a vampire but is not one of the immortal undead, at least not as far as that tradition is concerned. Instead, Flagg simply exists; he appears without reason, engages in his game of destruction and despair, and disappears when the game turns against him. At the end, Larry Underwood watches the Dark Man closely as Trashcan Man approaches with the atomic device.

111

Larry senses something monstrous standing in front of where Flagg had stood, something "slumped and hunched and almost without shape--something with enormous yellow eyes slit by dark cat's pupils" (766) . . . and then the shape disappears, reminiscent of the manta-like darkness that erupts from the Presidential Suite in The Shining.

Randall Flagg, King clearly states, cannot be explained or defined. He is not the devil; nor is he werewolf or vampire or ghost. The most one can say is that he manifests the Black power, as he will do later in The Eyes of the Dragon.

In The Stand, King depends upon imagery to develop the struggle between Black and White. The Dark Man, of course, presents the Black; but the symbolic overtones attain a higher complexity in the novel. In a dream, Frannie perceives the Black force. She sees a tablecloth moving toward her:

> It wasn't her father under there.
> And what was under there was not dead.
>   Something--someone--filled with dark life and hideous good cheer was under there . . . (163)

Five hundred pages later, King enters into the dying mind of Harold Lauder to find memories of Moby Dick being written in long hand, along with The Scarlet Letter and Paradise Lost. The reference to Milton's epic echoes throughout The Stand, not only in narrative terms of a confrontation between ultimate good and ultimate evil but in more specific stylistic terms. King's comments about Tolkien of the most intriguing characters in The Stand recall that same complication. Randall Flagg fascinates. Trashcan Man moves with a febrile energy unlike anyone else in the novel. Lloyd Henreid may seem rat-like, but he has entered into levels of darkness that elevate his smallness beyond expectation (and even he knows this). Even more complex are characters like Harold Lauder and Nadine Cross, initially capable of great things but later choosing the darkness.

This complexity parallels King's choice of symbols. Extending the oxymoron implicit in "dark life" and "hideous good cheer" and capitalizing on a technique Milton exploited in the "darkness visible" and related images in Paradise Lost, King

This complexity parallels King's choice of symbols. Extending the oxymoron implicit in "dark life" and "hideous good cheer" and capitalizing on a technique Milton exploited in the "darkness visible" and related images in Paradise Lost, King conflates White with Black. Mother Abagail, spiritual leader of the White force, is black . . . proudly, stridently, intensely Black. Nadine Cross, on the other hand, reverses the image; as she consummates her relationship with the Dark Man, her hair turns starkly white. King is not satisfied with a Star Wars level of symbolic interpretation, with Luke Skywalker in white and Darth Vader in black. While there may indeed be a conflict between White and Black, the terminators between the two may blur, just as the boundaries between reality and unreality, rationality and irrationality, truth and falsehood blur throughout King's novels.

Many themes and images King uses elsewhere recur in The Stand. Sexuality appears as a threat, as it did in Carrie, Rage, Firestarter and a number of short stories. Frannie's pregnancy signals her entrance into the adult world while coinciding with an external threat to humanity itself. The perverted sexuality shared by Nadine Cross and Harold Lauder reflects their decision to join the Black; neither feels fulfillment through their actions. Ultimately, their union destroys both of them.

On the other hand, King acknowledges the rejuvenative force of sexuality as well. Frannie's child is the first to survive birth into the new world. In the strictest sense, The Stand transmutes from tragedy into comedy; according to classical definitions, the birth of a child can be sufficient to overcome a flood of sorrow and death. By closing the novel with Frannie, Stuart, and their son safely on their way back to Maine, King emphasizes the positive values of adulthood and sexuality. There may be more horror in store for humanity; after all, others may find bombs that will lead to radiation and sickness and death. But for now, there is regeneration and peace and rest.

The Stand also incorporates allusions to contemporary politics, as do so many of King's other narratives. Again, the allusions are ambivalent.

Power and politics are deadly. "We used to watch
Presidents decay before our very eyes from month
to month and even week to week on national TV,"
the Judge recalls, adding "except for Nixon, of
course, who thrives on power the way that a vampire bat thrives on blood" (387-388). Connecting
Nixon even imagistically with vampires reinforces
the attitudes toward politics common in King´s
fiction. That sense expands as King details
Boulder´s emergence into a re-creation of contemporary society. When Stuart Redman returns from
Las Vegas, he finds things changed: sheriffs carry
weapons, laws have begun to encroach on individual
liberty.

But the obverse is also true. Without law,
without the Constitution and Bill of Rights at the
foundation of Boulder as a community, without
sheriffs and jails, Boulder would not have been
able to stand against the Dark Man. For every
vampiric politician, there is a Judge, ready to
sacrifice all to insure the survival of Boulder
and its opposition to the dark. As with sexuality, there are no clear, easy distinctions;
politics is potentially both good and evil. The
individual must choose which it is to be.

Even the atomic weapons that figure so prominently in the conclusion of the novel are ambiguous. Clearly intended as an image of evil in the
hands of the Dark Man, the atomic device itself
becomes a mystical focus of power. As Trashcan
Man brings the device into Las Vegas, his physical
state indicates that a critical change has taken
place; he is literally a walking dead man, appearing "like some grim vision out of a horror tale"
(765). As Flagg confronts Trashcan, the Dark Man
suddenly becomes "the pale man" (766), the electrical bolt he had himself released turns against
him. Forming the shape of a gigantic hand, the
power sweeps down to touch the device. As Lloyd
Henreid screams his fear and Larry Underwood reit-
erates his faith, the bomb explodes: "And the
righteous and the unrighteous alike were consumed
in that holy fire" (767).

The bomb destroys, but it also cleanses.

As impressive as the scene is, however, the
destruction of Las Vegas is not the climactic moment in The Stand. As the name implies, the novel
concentrates on the moment of decision each indi-

114

vidual makes, whether to stand with the White or with the Black. The amgibuities of theme and image suggest that the decisions cannot be made easily, nor can one individual decide for another. What brings regeneration and peace to one can destroy another. Glen Bateman's reactions to meeting the Dark Man face to face may in fact provide the closest thing to a single moment of climax. Secure in his own decisions, Bateman can look in the face of evil and laugh (753). Bateman penetrates Flagg's pretentions, sees the lack of substance beneath the surface horror, and laughs. Death holds no fear for Bateman. Echoing Christ's words from the cross, Bateman whispers, "It's all right, Mr. Henreid . . . You don't know any better" (754).

The Stand is powerful, one of King's most teachable works. It is not perfect, of course. Many readers find the length and complex inter-weaving of characters difficult; one can only wonder what reactions would have been had the en-tire manuscript been published. Style occasional-ly jars with context, as when Tom Cullen recites the Lord's Prayer. He gets the first lines right, then slips into an oddly distracting diction: "He greases up my head with oil. He gives me kung-fu in the face of my enemies" (704). Later, in describing Trashcan Man just before the atomic blast, King notes that he had never "flagged" in his determination (767). While there is nothing inherently inappropriate about the pun, the posi-tioning seems at best awkward.

In spite of the potential problems, however, The Stand remains ambitious and satisfying. While it may be intriguing to see where materials were deleted, should an unexpurgated version ever make it through the layers of contractual disputes that have delayed it so far, the novel as published stands on its own. In terms of moving beyond the narrow limits of horror fiction, The Stand indi-cates what King is capable of; in The Dark Tower, The Eyes of the Dragon, and The Talisman he ampli-fies those powers.

The Dark Tower

While The Dark Tower: The Gunslinger does not overtly continue the adventures of Randall Flagg

115

in tangential worlds, it connects with structural and thematic elements in The Stand, specifically through the atmosphere of apocalypse pervading the five stories. Although King never defines explicit relationships between our world and the world of the Gunslinger, he suggests a science fictional time-displacement that allows characters to move from one to another. The boy Jake dies in what appears to be our world, only to reappear at the way station in time to meet the Gunslinger, accompany him on part of his quest, and make possible the climactic meeting with the Dark Man.

The Dark Man also moves between worlds, slipping into Jake's reality to orchestrate the boy's death, returning to tempt Roland into the wilderness as part of a grander plan associated with the Dark Tower, the three, and a restoration of time and space. While the opening fragment King gives us in The Dark Tower: The Gunslinger does not even define clearly the final quest, it strongly suggests both the wasted world of The Stand and the alternative worlds King would develop in The Eyes of the Dragon and The Talisman.

The gunslinger's name, Roland, links The Dark Tower with The Eyes of the Dragon. In both, King concentrates on the dissolution of kingdoms through the machinations of evil incarnate: Marten's manipulations of the Lord of Light in the first, Flagg's control over and eventual murder of another Roland in the second. The court scenes in both works are near enough in broad details to be re-constructions of the same world--as if King's years-long work with the Dark Tower stories stimulated Eyes. It seems feasible that eventually, additional narratives could link the two; at least twice in Eyes, King hints of new tales to be told, of new encounters between humans and the faceless man, Flagg.

As fascinating and frustrating as The Dark Tower is (see SW 99-118), it is of interest here primarily as an early sketch for the alternative worlds, balanced between reality and fantasy, at the center of The Eyes of the Dragon and The Talisman. In these two novels, published in 1984, King refines his interest in high fantasy as he creates a "wonderful/terrible tour" of lands that never were (Philtrum).

The Eyes of the Dragon

The Eyes of the Dragon has stirred up controversy since the announcement of its forthcoming
publication. Since Philtrum limited the press run
to 1,000 copies (plus 250 copies printed in red
ink and reserved for the author), demand for the
book intensified even before its appearance in
late 1984, in spite of the original $120 price.
As recently as March, 1985, Philtrum was still
working out details of the lottery system that
would allow as much objectivity as possible in
distributing copies; at the same time, the price
among collectors and dealers had reached $350. By
September, 1985, well within a year of its publication, Eyes was being offered at figures ranging
from $650 to $800, with at least one astronomical
bid of $1200--while many readers were still un-
aware of its existence at all.

George Beahm's "Collecting Stephen King Limiteds" and King's "The Politics of Limited Editions" discuss reactions to this publication
arrangement, the first from a reader's perspective, the second from the author's. King's
responses are particularly important in this case,
since there is a close connection between King and
Philtrum Press. Charles De Lint's review refers
to Eyes as the "first book from a new publishing
company"; the descriptive bibliography in Fear
Itself, however, lists The Plant among King's
books, noting that it was published by Philtrum as
"the opening segment of an ongoing work" (255),
which King has identified as IT. My own corre-
spondence with Philtrum confirms the close link
with King; the signator of one letter was Shirley
Sonderegger, secretary to Stephen King and Philtrum Press. The limited appearance of Eyes seems,
then, a considered action on King's part, with him
determining at least in part both cost and press
run. For all but King collectors and completists,
however, the issue will become moot within the
next year or so; The Eyes of the Dragon is one of
four novels scheduled for trade release between
1986 and 1987.

Those among King's fans who have not yet read
Eyes have a pleasant experience in store; it is
among his best, self-consistent, understated at
times, tightly plotted and exciting. Originally

intended as a children's story, <u>Eyes</u> speaks as well to adults, approaching the universality of the finest children's literature. At the same time, it develops the intimacy of a story-teller speaking to a rapt audience. Only occasionally does King allow an intrusive word, phrase, or image to break the spell he weaves; most of the distractions are on the level of crudities--"snot" or "booger" or "turd"--rather than the harsher language many readers expect from him. For the most part, as De Lint says, he

> concentrates on the people, on how the events of the story affect their lives. There is little magic, except for that used by Flagg, but the book retains a sense of wonder that too many current fantasy novels lack. It has, as well, sibling rivalry, regicide, a doomed prince in a tower, an off-stage dragon, and appearances by Peter Straub's son Ben and King's own daughter Naomi in supporting roles--the latter as a spunky, cigar-chomping dog-sled driver. The voice of the book is that of an oral story-teller's, straight-forward, yet with a lyricism that will surprise many King detractors.

<u>Eyes</u> shows what King can do without the shock value of obscenity, strongly arguing that when such language does appear--as in <u>Christine</u>, for example--it does so for specific purposes. The bluntness that has led many readers to question King's language, it seems, is a conscious part of the narrative structure where it occurs. Given the audience and the genre of <u>Eyes</u>, that language would be inappropriate, and King avoids it.

Originally, King referred to the novel as <u>The Napkins</u>, a title pointing directly to a specific point in the narrative. As the narrator frequently reminds his readers (perhaps "listeners" is a better term, since part of the fiction of <u>Eyes</u> is the sense of the narrator telling a bedtime story to children), Peter insists upon using napkins. When the imprisoned Prince requests napkins with each meal, they become more central, culminating with the escape itself. Still, there is a juvenile

sense to the title, a suggestion of something
light and almost frivolous.

The title King finally chose for publication,
however, has broader ties with the narrative. The
Eyes of the Dragon refers to the "off-stage dragon" killed by King Roland and mounted on the wall
of his private chamber. Through the yellow-green
faceted eyes, Flagg and Thomas spy on Roland, and
Thomas sees Flagg poison the King. Because so
much of the narrative uses convoluted flashbacks,
frequently involving the eyes of Niner, the later
title fits nicely. Imagistically, it is more satisfying as well. When Thomas looks through the
eyes of the dragon, he sees everything tinged with
the yellow-green cast of the eyes. After his
first experience in the hidden chamber behind the
dragon´s head, Thomas feels ill because, as he
tells himself, "you were seeing the way dragons
must see the world--as if everything was dried out
and ready to burn" (77). The colors are signifi-
cant; again and again in King´s fiction, yellow or
green eyes are associated with monsters, with
aliens, with evil itself (SK/RB 143).

Thomas does in fact see things through a
dragon´s perceptions; Flagg, the incarnation of
evil incessantly associated with smoke and fumes
and yellow-green fire, colors what Thomas sees and
thinks. Like Harold Lauder in The Stand (and the
parallels between the two are frequent and insistent), Thomas pivots between two worlds. He has
the potential for great good or great evil; his
choice will determine not only his own fate but
the fate of his kingdom. And like Harold Lauder,
Thomas proves a weak vessel. Even knowing that
Peter is innocent of patricide and that Flagg is
in fact guilty, Thomas allows fear and pride and
greed and little-mindedness to sway his actions.
He remains silent, thereby condemning himself to
tortures of conscience, his brother to five years
imprisonment in a cell, and his kingdom to increasing disorder and danger. By seeing through
the eyes of the dragon that Flagg is, Thomas
becomes a paradoxically passive agent of chaos and
disorder.

On another level, the eyes of the dragon seem
even more important to the narrative. In the
final confrontation with Flagg, beneath the head
of Niner and within view of its yellow-green eyes,

Thomas finally sees clearly. Dressed in his
father's robe, holding his father's weapons,
sitting in his father's chair, he decides to speak
truth, breaking the spell Flagg has woven around
him and the Kingdom of Delain. He shoots Foe-
Hammer, the great arrow. It strikes Flagg's eye,
the eye of another kind of dragon, as destructive
as old Niner but malevolent and unnatural. As in
The Stand, Flagg disappears. Evil cannot be destroyed, but it can be disrupted.

Flagg's presence in the novel is one of the
most remarkable things about it. In an interview
with David Sherman, King spoke of the forthcoming
novel as

> a book-length comic, almost like a fairy
> tale. And the bad guy in that book is
> Randall Flagg. His name's changed a
> little bit, but his last name's the
> same--Flagg. It's him! He turned up in
> this other book. In this other world.
> (20)

Flagg connects The Eyes of the Dragon with The
Stand, and by doing so emphasizes the other-
worldliness of the story. The narrator constantly
cross-references between the world of Delain and
the world of his listeners. The "featherex," we
are told, is Delain's analogue to our Phoenix
(75). Delain's inhabitants fear the Baby Death
(54) and Wet Lung (55); we have crib death and
pneumonia.

Yet the narrator also goes out of his way to
establish the "reality" of Delain. The novel may
be, as King commented, "almost like a fairy tale,"
but if so, the operant word is almost. Magic
exists in Delain, but a carefully controlled and
circumscribed magic; as the narrator says, "real
magic is hard, and although it is easier to do
evil magic than good, even bad magic is tolerably
hard" (61). The traditional fairy tale ending is
conspicuous by its absence; although Eyes begins
with a variant on the formulaic "once upon a
time," even to the equally conventional figure of
the King with two sons, the conclusion explicitly
denies the fairy tale:

> Did they all live happily ever af-

ter?

They did not. No one ever does, in
spite of what the fairy tales may say.
(312)

More importantly, the narrator consistently refers
to fairy tale motifs as similes and metaphors, as
vehicles for understanding rather than the things
themselves. As Dennis tells his story to Ben and
Naomi, they listen "as spellbound as children
hearing the tale of the talking wolf in the
gammer´s nightgown" (271). The great storm that
engulfs Delain (as external conditions mirror
inner turmoil and chaos) blows over farmhouses as
easily as "the wolf´s hungry breath in the old
story" (274). And Castle Delain is twice referred
to as a "fairy-tale castle" (221).

It is as if the narrator were forcing his
listeners to discriminate between reality and fantasy, between his narrative and the fairy tale.
Delain may not exist in our world but it does
exist. There may be magic but not the simplistic
magic of fairy-tales. There may have been dragons
once but now they are dead; the only "dragons"
left are men made evil and perverse by the power
of Darkness.

Additionally, the narrator frequently creates
moments of hesitation. One definition of fantasy
notes that the characters (and the reader) undergo
an experience that requires a decision: either an
inexplicable event actually occurred, in which
case the characters must re-formulate their understanding of reality to account for ghosts, vampires, or other intrusions of the irrational; or
it did not occur, and the characters have
experienced a hallucination of some sort but the
laws of the universe remain intact.   Only during
the moment of hesitation, when the characters have
not yet decided which explanation is correct, can
the fantastic exist, according to Tzvetan Todorov.

The narrator of _Eyes_ frequently uses this
technique, creating an interesting texture of
uncertainty as he provides the listeners with two
explanations for a given event, one entirely possible and one requiring magic or the supernatural.
Each time, the narrator refuses to choose between
the two, leaving the final decision up to his listeners and by doing so creating precisely the sort

121

of hesitation that Todorov defines.   Dennis does
not enter the sewer pipes   still   contaminated by
the Dragon Sand; had he done so he would have died
and the story would have had a different ending.
But whether luck, fate, or the gods saved him, the
narrator refuses to say.   Peter, Anders Peyna,
Dennis, Ben, and Naomi all feel that things are
moving to a crisis; whether their sense of urgency
resulted from assessing events in Delain or from
the movement of deeper powers within them,   again
the narrator does not say. Instead he forces his
characters´ uncertainty and hesitation upon his
listeners.

     That hesitation is crucial to the text.   As
in The Stand, the confrontation in Eyes takes
place between the forces of White and the forces
of Black. Some of the characters are obviously
allied with one side or the other.   Flagg, of
course, represents archetypal darkness, even to
his ability to become "dim," his hiding his face
in shadow, his living in deep darkness beneath the
Castle. Others belong to the White: Peter, always
valiant, never despairing, never falling for any
of Flagg´s strategems--always and ever the true
Prince and rightful King. At the risk of drawing
too specific an analogy, he is Peter the Rock,
true heir to the kingdom, tempted, tested, and
triumphant. Imprisoned at the top of the Tower, he
is imagistically Christ-like, as high as Flagg is
low in the dungeon-like chambers; even in his isolation, Peter discovers the locket that leads in
part to Flagg´s undoing. Ben Staad and Naomi
Reechul (already mentioned as reflecting Peter
Straub´s son and King´s daughter) are equally
steadfast, never doubting.   Anders Peyna stands
for law and justice, even when those decisions
bring pain. Later, as he understands how completely the Black has subverted law, he stands
just as adamantly for justice in the face of law,
restoring order and avoiding chaos. (His name,
incidentally, suggests the Spanish "pena," with
its overtones of embarrassment. Peyna is embar-
rassed, caught up by his own pride and ridiculed
by an inner voice for his part in Peter´s trial
[219, 222]; but that flaw does not keep him from
fighting for right, even at his own expense).

     Between the extremes stands Thomas. Just as
in The Stand, the central action in Eyes consists

of a series of choices by individuals. Evil is
not overturned by a single heroic act; Roland´s
slaying of the dragon Niner, for example, does not
rid the land of danger, as it might have in a more
traditional fairy tale. Instead, each person is
tested. Within each person, King says, struggle
the desire for good and the desire for "blackness
and secrets" (126). The strong hold firm; the
weak falter, and Flagg either destroys them or
marks them for destruction.

As the beneficiary of Roland´s death and
Peter´s imprisonment, Thomas undergoes special
temptation. Already weak and frustrated by his
father´s preference for Peter, Thomas develops
into another Harold Lauder, fat and marked by
pimples, his outward appearance an accurate
indication of his inner failings. He is not evil,
the narrator assures us (and we believe him), but
he is weak. And he is the king.

Thomas tries once to assert himself, but almost immediately falls to Flagg´s persuasions. He
joins the side of the Black. In an imagistic inversion reminiscent of King´s treatment of Mother
Abagail (the leader of the White is black) and
Nadine Cross (the bride of the Dark Man has white
hair), the boy becomes Thomas the Light-Bringer,
destined to immerse Delain in greater darkness
than it has ever known. Again, the name is symbolic. "Light-bringer" could translate as "Luci-
fer," the name of the son of the morning who led a
third of heaven´s hosts with him into hell. When
King conflates "Light-Bringer" with "Tax-Bringer"
(179), he signals Flagg´s near-absolute control
over Thomas.

Eyes ends more optimistically than The Stand,
however. Harold Lauder is destroyed by the darkness he chooses; Thomas, on the other hand, retains enough of his humanity to stand against
Flagg. Like a "doubting Thomas" juxtaposed to
Peter the Rock, he never forgets what he has seen
or his distrust and fear of Flagg, in spite of
momentary vacillations. When the critical moment
arrives, as Flagg moves to destroy Peter and his
supporters, Thomas speaks up, acknowledges his own
guilt, and destroys Flagg´s physical shape. The
tool Flagg has prepared to disrupt Delain turns on
Flagg instead; as the narrator says several times
in the novel, evil ultimately defeats itself by

123

its own intricate machinations. The essence of evil escapes, as it did from the Overlook in The Shining, but Thomas has earned his own restitution. Through him, Peter returns to the throne.

The Eyes of the Dragon, like so many of King's works, reaches beyond itself to touch other novels. Frisky, the dog who tracks Dennis to Castle Delain and makes it possible for Ben and Naomi to save Peter's life, reminds us of the sane Cujo, even down to the way King re-creates the dog's thoughts. Flagg's mad ravings as he climbs the three hundred stairs to Peter's cell recall Jack Torrance's threats to Danny: "Here I come, Peter . . . . Here I come, dear Peter, to do what I should have done a long, long time ago" (287). (In fact, King's descriptions of Flagg struggling up and down the steps, battle-axe in hand, shattering doors and skulls, may owe as much to Jack Nicholson's interpretation of Torrance in Kubrick's The Shining as to any other single source, an interesting possibility for an influence from film back to text.) The Stand contributes not only Flagg but also a number of details that bring the world of Delain to life: blue fire from Flagg's fingertips; the analogue to Harold Lauder; monitory dreams that afflict both the good and the evil.

In addition, Eyes alludes to two seminal fantasists. Lovecraft appears only tangentially, in a reference to a book "written on the high, distant Plains of Leng by a madman named Alhazred" (60). Still, there is a faintly Lovecraftian sense about the novel, particularly in the episodes in Flagg's chambers as he delves into forbidden knowledge and eldritch secrets.

Tolkien, on the other hand, contributes several important touches to Eyes. The great arrow Foe-Hammer, dragon-bane and destroyer of evil, recalls Tolkien's elven sword. Dennis's experiences in the fields west of Castle Delain similarly recall Frodo's on the high seat of kings in The Lord of the Rings; in each instance, the character senses the eye of evil passing over him as it casts outward in its restlessness. Even more importantly, in both The Lord of the Rings and The Eyes of the Dragon, evil cannot be permanently defeated. Sauron is, after all, only a discorporate force in Tolkien's tale, physically destroyed

eons before by Isuldur, now once again spreading
his darkness outward from Mordor. The destruction
of the Ring of Power cripples him but does not
destroy him entirely. Flagg is similarly more
elemental force than human. He has endured for
centuries, suffering momentary setbacks at the
hands of a Valera, a Kyla the Good, a Sasha, or a
Peter; he may be forced from Delain, but his
influence remains.

The parallels with Tolkien also explain the
elegaic ending of Eyes. Although repentant and
contrite, Thomas is wise enough to realize that he
has no place in Delain; even under Peter's protection, he would be in danger from a populace infur-
iated by his actions as King. So Thomas leaves.
In a scene remarkably reminiscent of Frodo's fare-
well to Hobbiton at the beginning of The Lord of
the Rings, Thomas sets out on his own quest to
find Flagg. Like Frodo, he too is accompanied by
a simple rustic, Dennis, a character who makes up
in loyalty and perseverance what he might lack in
intellect. And, as the narrator says in closing,

> Thomas and Dennis had many strange ad-
> ventures, and . . . they did see Flagg
> again, and confront him.
>   But now the hour is late, and all
> of that is another tale, for another
> day. (314).

Delain has changed. Even without Flagg's
physical presence, it suffers the depredations of
evil and darkness. Peter remains behind; his duty
is to be King, to reign long and well and restore
order. But Thomas cannot stay. Like Frodo at the
conclusion of The Lord of the Rings, he has been
through too much, has suffered too much, and has
no place in the new world. There are important
differences, of course; Frodo was a Ring-bearer
and Gandalf's ally, while Thomas had accepted
Flagg's evil passively, if not willingly. But at
the end, the heroic surfaces, and Thomas sets
forth on his own quest.

The Eyes of the Dragon establishes King's
ability to make his own way, not only in "contemporary thrillers and dark fantasy," to quote De
Lint, but in high fantasy as well. The novel
stands on its own as an engaging narrative; and at

the same time, it bridges King´s two most ambitious fictions, The Stand and The Talisman, bringing new depths of meaning to each.

The Talisman

Alan Warren´s "Has Success Spoiled Stephen King?" approaches the knotty question of commercialism and artistic integrity, noting that of the ten novels published under King´s own name after Carrie, only two deserve oblivion: The Dark Tower and The Talisman (16).

Unfortunately for both books, Warren´s is not an isolated criticism; but the reactions to the latter novel do tend to greater stridency and harshness than the responses to The Dark Tower. That, after all, was an admitted experiment, a beginning toward a grander vision perhaps not possible to capture on paper. The Talisman, on the other hand, was the work of two accomplished novelists who, according to a number of critics, should have known better.

Charles Leerhsen´s review in Newsweek epitomizes this reaction. After several paragraphs devoted to backgrounds, Leerhsen launches into his critique. Viking has distributed a record one million hardcover copies of the book, he notes,

> meaning that many people who normally
> get books for Christmas will instead get
> "Talismans." No one who wears glasses
> is absolutely safe, and those who do can
> start practicing their frozen smiles
> ("Gee, thanks, Aunt Sophie!"). (61)

Later, he refers to Straub as seeming "as unphony as the $3 bill he and his collaborator split for each book." When he actually discusses the novel itself, his tone and language leave no question as to his attitude: the "jarring plot-twists that King and Straub are famous for are, in this case, telegraphed meathandedly"; the novel is almost "glacial" in pace; and it reads like a novelization of a film (61).

After a single paragraph discussing the literary merits (or demerits) of The Talisman, he moves again into the realms of publicity budgets and the details of composition.

Leerhsen´s approach emphasizes the unevenness of responses to the novel. Hailed as a landmark by two leading writers, it was simultaneously condemned roundly (even before publication) for being commercial, exploitative, and (worse yet!) boring. King has cited a review in People magazine that read: "Watch out for these guys, they have written two of the worst novels of 1983 on their own, and in 1984, they are teaming up to do a book together" (cited in Winter, "Quest" 68). After The Talisman appeared, People published an additional note. The "Worst of Pages" section of the "Picks & Pans" column comments that "in horror fiction, two heads are better than one only if they´re on the same body" (24-31 December 1984).

Yet like each of King´s recent novels, The Talisman swept to the top of national bestsellers lists, recouping Viking´s publicity budget in the first day of sale. Within a month of the "Picks & Pans" note, People devoted three pages to "America´s current No. 1 best-seller," calling it a "644-page fantasy about a 12-year-old boy´s odyssey in a netherworld filled with vicious werewolves and killer trees"--at best a skewed representation of the novel, concentrating on minor characteristics that occur within the first 150 pages and suggesting closer affinities to Tolkien than actually exist. Still, the article claims, it is a "triumph of terror" (Small 51).

A number of situations might account for this extraordinary diversity of opinions.

Several are external. The authors´ reputations might have made it difficult for either to gain a fair hearing from mainstream reviewers, particularly in light of the influx of films from King´s novels over the preceding year, King´s publication of The Eyes of the Dragon less than two months after The Talisman, and the increasingly solid rumors about Thinner, published in the same month as Eyes.

In addition, the publication arrangements for the novel were themselves extreme, inviting both skepticism and charges of overt commercialism. Even before publication, booksellers advertised the novel at a reduced, advance-order rate. Then, in one of the largest press runs in publishing history, Viking printed 600,000 copies, with 502,000 sequestered in secret warehouses around the country, including General Electric distribution centers. On publication day, October 8, 1984, all half million plus were released simultaneously, creating the illusion of a flooded market ("502,000 Copies" 25). Outlets could almost literally cover their walls with The Talisman in its distinctive black, red, and yellow dust jacket.

As impressive as the distribution system was --and Daniel W. Murphy, executive vice-president of Publishers Shipping Cooperative Association called it a "milestone" for the industry--it also created a visual over-kill; seeing stacks and stacks of novels in bookstore after bookstore for weeks afterward almost defeated the purpose of the arrangements in the first place. Nevertheless, the initial run of 600,000 sold out, as did a second run of 75,000; recent records indicate over one million copies in print.

To add fuel to the fire, advertisements for the book announced that it would not be available through Book Clubs; readers would have to pay full cover price of $18.95. In an interview with Paul S. Nathan of Publishers Weekly, King defended the decision:

> Once your books sell a certain number of copies . . . you become important as an instrument to bring in future members. Not that present members won't buy your book, but membership turnover is high and your book becomes one of those where people say, "I really want to read that and I don't want to wait for the paperback." They can join and get four books for a dollar. If the Guild is going to do this, they should be required to pay for it.

In this case, "pay for it" meant increasing the Guild's offer of $400,000 to $700,000, which the Guild declined to do. King insists that he is not opposed to Book Club editions; Skeleton Crew, published after The Talisman, will be offered through the Book-of-the-Month Club. "Clubs are an integral part of the industry," King continues in the interview. "I'm not out to bust them. But I think the climate that spawned clubs has changed

128

radically" (28).

As if the unusual distribution arrangements
and the furor over Club sales were not enough,
King and Straub also had to contend with a back-
lash stemming from the sale of film rights to
Steven Spielberg. Some reviewers saw the negotiations as another way to capitalize on the authors´
inordinate popularity. People spoke of the novel
being "snapped up" by Spielberg (Small 51).
Leerhsen´s article was more critical; the book
reads like a novelization, he says,

> a charge that Straub finds "obscene"--
> the authors´ just-completed deal with
> Universal Pictures and Steven Spielberg
> notwithstanding. (61)

A film contract for a King novel (or even a Straub
novel) should raise few eyebrows; by the time The
Talisman appeared, film versions of almost every
book published under King´s name (plus two of the
Bachman novels) were either completed, in production, or planned. That a work the magnitude of
The Talisman might come to the attention of one of
the premier names in fantasy films seems understandable. The negotiations were long and difficult, primarily because Spielberg wanted to work
with the novel in spite of a number of other
projects; he was, as King puts it, "determined to
have his own way about this . . ." (Wiater and
Anker 12). Given the intensely visual sense King
has developed in his novels over the past decade,
it is as if The Talisman were being faulted for
succeeding in precisely what it set out to do.

In addition to these external complications,
there are a number of internal difficulties as
well.

To begin with, reviewers have charged that
the novel is too long. The complaint stems in
part from an abuse by some writers who, as Parke
Godwin says, give readers "seven hundred pages of
a three-hundred page book." The reader, he
argues, will resent such an intrusion, in spite of
the current popularity of verbosity. Concerned
about the trend to longer novels afflicted with
"literary elephantiasis" (a term King uses as well
to define his own style), Godwin suggests that
readers have undergone a change in standards, from

the "time of faster-paced drama and prose" Godwin recalls to

> an attempted return to the indulgent
> rambling of the nineteenth century with-
> out the Victorian values or the subtle
> craft of, say, a James or Le Fanu. Evi-
> dently this new generation of readers
> will sit and digest 750 flabbily written
> pages without cavil. Certainly they'll
> sit through a space opera too long by
> forty-five minutes of visuals if there's
> big Dolby sound and a John Williams
> score soaring and sobbing from the
> speakers. Or a decayed corpse or two in
> close-up just to keep things gemütlich-
> keit [sic]. (11)

The reason, he concludes, may stem from television; readers babysat by television when they
were children may have transferred a willingness
to follow simple action to their reading.

Godwin does not mention King specifically;
nor does he need to. It is almost a critical com-
monplace that King's novels are frequently longer
than the plot requires. Some have estimated that
Christine is a third longer than necessary; passages in "Apt Pupil" might be shortened. The
Stand, long as it is (823 pages in the Doubleday
hardcover) was pared by 20% from King's manuscript. And, as noted above, King himself recognizes the wordiness in his style ("Afterword" to
SC, 508).

This is not to suggest, however, that King
simply indulges himself in a technique he finds
questionable. Quite the contrary. King addressed
the issue in "Love Those Long Books," one of his
reviews for Adelina (November 1980). Ostensibly
about the Dover reprint of Wilkie Collins' No
Name, the article argues:

> There was an age--it ended around 1950,
> I should judge--when the long novel was
> accepted on its own terms and judged
> upon matters other than its length:
> there was a time before that when the
> long novel was the rule rather than the
> exception. Since 1950--about the time

that these same mainline critics finished walling poetry off from the greater
mass of American readers by convincing
them they couldn't understand it--the
novel has been more and more discrimin-
ated against on the grounds of length
alone. Many critics seem to take a novel of more than 400 pages as a personal
affront.

One such critic, he notes, wished that the author
of The Dead Zone had developed a "case of perma-
nent dyslexia"; another said of The Stand that
"Given enough rope, any writer will hang himself
. . . and in this novel, King has taken enough
rope to outfit an entire clipper ship."
    Even granting a certain defensiveness in the
Adelina review, it seems clear that King approaches the craft of storytelling from a radically
different angle than many of his detractors. His
imagined worlds, however close they may be to what
his readers consider reality, require careful con-
struction. The intrusion of the supernatural
works most effectively against a solidly struc-
tured illusion of reality; if The Stand intends to
convince its readers that Randall Flagg exists,
the fact of his essentially irrational and supernatural nature may require a meticulously built up
background. In The Talisman, King and Straub must
make not only our world believable, but the Territories as well--and at the same time convince the
reader that sufficient time has passed for the
episodes in the narrative to be credible. Much of
Moby Dick (to refer to a nineteenth-century example) could be considered extraneous to the
straight plot line; a number of non-narrative
chapters seem as important for creating a sense of
temporal duration as for moving the plot forward.
    Other complaints about The Talisman seem out-
growths of the first: it is a collaboration by two
"Big Names," and therefore almost automatically a
target for sharpshooters. Even before publication, it was optioned by a film producer whose
commercial successes have made history. It is
long--designedly so--and therefore "glacial," te-
dious, or boring.
    On the other hand, a number of objections to
The Talisman ignore one important element: genre.

131

Readers coming to the novel expecting more of what they found in Christine, Pet Sematary, Shadowland or Floating Dragon are bound to be disappointed, just as readers approaching Tolkien's Silmarillion expecting a reprise of The Lord of the Rings will be disappointed.

The comparison is apt and important. In both instances, the authors shift genres, radically and fundamentally. In spite of the presence of elves and wizards in The Silmarillion, it does not just continue The Lord of the Rings. Instead, it is a creation epic, requiring different techniques and structures. Vocabulary and narrative voice change; episodes become more abstracted and generalized; time dilates; length becomes a matter of creating the illusion of eons passing, rather than merely months or years. This is not to say that either approach is necessarily better, only that they are different, with different ends, different characteristics, different effects on the readers.

The same situation exists in The Talisman. Warren's comparison of the novel with The Dark Tower is appropriate in at least one sense: both represent King moving away from the traditions and expectations he has established for himself. Both blend the surface characteristics of horror or dark fantasy with the structures, purposes, and tones of epic quest and high fantasy. To condemn the novels for succeeding in what they attempted, while failing in what they carefully eschewed, seems unreasonable and unfair.

The question of genre is particularly important in The Talisman since it encompasses so much, becoming virtually an encyclopedia of possibilities as it explores science fiction, fantasy, horror, and fairy tale.

Most immediately, it entails alternate universe fiction in the reciprocality between Jack Sawyer's world and the Territories, yet Morgan Sloat refers to Phil Sawyer's story of another world as "science-fiction crapola" (70). And in spite of frequent references to science fiction, particularly in the form of similes, the novel rejects many of its key elements, critiquing that genre as it does others. In the final third, Richard Sloat becomes increasingly important, even though he has rejected "any sort of fantasy, even science fiction"; Jack comments that "techies"

such as Richard usually consumed large quantities
of Heinlein, Asimov, Clarke, or Niven, while
avoiding the "metaphysical bullshit" of a Malzberg
or a Silverberg (412). What surprises him is that
Richard seems incapable of accepting any representation of paranormal reality, no matter how firmly
based in scientific fact or technological innova-
tion. As Jack's quest for the talisman becomes
Richard's as well, it also becomes a means of
expanding Richard's imagination as it expands the
reader's. Whatever The Talisman is, it is not
traditional science fiction; instead, it more
closely resembles Piers Anthony's conflation of
science fiction and fantasy in the Proton/Phaze
novels, Split Infinity, Blue Adept, and Juxtaposi-
tion, in which alternate worlds serve as analogues
to each other, one based on science and rationality, the other on magic and the fantastic. What
elements of science fiction exist in The Talisman
relate best to what C. S. Lewis termed mythopoeic
fiction. In "On Science Fiction," Lewis defined
five sub-types of the genre, the fifth and last
being the most important and for Lewis the only
valid sort, derived from a "wish to visit strange
regions in search of such beauty, awe, or terror
as the actual world does not supply" (68).

Lewis's definition lies close to J. R. R.
Tolkien's in "On Fairy-Stories," as he discusses
the basic functions of fantasy: recovery, escape,
and consolation. Even more to the point, he introduces "Mooreeffoc, or Chestertonian fantasy."
The word is "fantastic," Tolkien says,

> but it could be seen written up in every
> town in this land. It is Coffee-room,
> viewed from the inside through a glass
> door, as it was seen by Dickens on a
> dark London day; and it was used by
> Chesterton to denote the queerness of
> things that have become trite, when they
> are seen suddenly from a new angle. (58)

Limited though this form of fantasy might be, it
relates to what King and Straub work toward in The
Talisman; early in the novel, in fact, Jack Sawyer
looks up and sees "DLROWNUF AIDACRA" written
against the sky (32)--a specifically mooreeffocian
moment. Later, as Jack Sawyer flips into the Ter-

133

ritories, he has "an experience of remarkable sensory impact, seeing and hearing and smelling things which were brand-new to him, while other sensory input to which he had grown utterly accustomed was missing for the first time" (189).

If King's earlier works were grounded in Poe and Lovecraft, The Talisman (as perhaps befits its collaborative composition) looks to other fantasists for its underlying imagery and patterns. References to Poe and Lovecraft are fewer and less critical than in other of King's works, functioning more as allusions than as structural or thematic devices. Instead, works such as Lewis's Narnia novels are deeply embedded in The Talisman, particularly as the narrative concentrates on an alternative world reached at first through magic and later through desire; the plot line of The Talisman in fact parallels the action of The Magician's Nephew closely--a young man moves into an alternate reality to find a talisman that will heal his dying mother. In doing so, he comes to understand his own reality more completely and confirms the need for right choice in both worlds; he learns simply to do a good thing.

King and Straub make no secret of how important Lewis and Tolkien were to the narrative conception of The Talisman. In addition to Straub's comment made in January of 1983 that The Talisman was "a quest novel with fantasy elements" and that it would "be the size of The Lord of the Rings if it goes on much longer," King and Straub incorporate allusions to Lewis and Tolkien throughout. The Lord of the Rings not only contributes references to Ents, for example, but also the tone of Jack's walking song. Appropriately enough, Wolf's terror in the shopping mall theater stems from Ralph Bakshi's version of The Lord of the Rings.

As a result, The Talisman seems in some ways a gentler work than either King or Straub usually offer. It is not without violence, cruelty, and terror, of course; Lewis and Tolkien also frequently crossed into similar territory. But even its most horrific moments seem touched with a quiet optimism. The episodes with Wolf at the Sunlight Home or Richard Sloat at Thayer School may include gruesome and horrifying elements, but they owe more to memories of Frodo and Sam on the trek to Mount Doom than to Ben Mears and Mark

Petrie battling vampires, particularly in the relationships Jack develops toward Wolf and Richard.
The Blasted Lands are closer to Tolkien´s dead
marshes than to Trashcan Man´s desert in The
Stand, in spite of references to radioactivity.
On the whole, The Talisman moves with a steadier,
more deliberate pace, its horrific episodes ameliorated by tone and treatment.

Even more importantly, the novel concentrates
on a key element in both Tolkien´s and Lewis´s
theories of the fantastic. Tolkien calls it the
"eucatastrophe," the consolation of the happy
ending. Lewis is more generalized, referring in
his critical and biographical works to "Joy," to
an emotion deeper than reason or logic. In The
Talisman, Jack Sawyer experiences both--explicitly
in the episode of the flying men in the Territories, who are sustained by an almost visible
joy; and implicitly in his desire for "moreness"
(385). There may be pain in Jack Sawyer´s world,
and loss and death; but there is also restoration.
Just as Frodo emerges from his quest changed, or
Ransom from his in Lewis´s space novels, Jack Sawyer is changed. He has the power to heal and uses
it wisely; in doing so, he heals himself as well.
Only in the final paragraphs of the novel does he
return to anything near what he was before.
Tolkien has his hobbit depart from the Grey Havens
with the elves and wizards; Lewis´s Ransom travels
to Perelandra to live with Arthur. Having accomplished his task, Jack Sawyer receives perhaps a
greater reward: through the power of the talisman,
he returns to his "ordinary life of school and
friends and games and music" (644).

In addition, the literary allusions that
color The Talisman also tend toward light fantasy.
Except for several paraphrases from Straub´s Shadowland ("When we all lived in California and no
one lived anywhere else. . ." [159]) and Floating
Dragon, or such occasional reminders from King´s
novels as the Rainbird Towers or the haunted Black
Hotel, readers are more likely to see echoes from
The Wizard of Oz than from The Colour Out of
Space, or "The Masque of the Red Death." The
image of George Romero´s shambling walking dead is
countered by the inherent comedy of An American
Werewolf in London as Wolf undergoes his transformation in a mall theater. Even the name "Jack

135

Sawyer" diverts the novel from horror. While the
first name might be construed as a backward glance
at Jack Torrance, the surname connects The Talisman with Mark Twain. Thomas Woodbine ("Uncle
Thomas") dies early, as if to insure more to the
book than a rehashing of Twain. Still, occasional
echoes lend The Talisman additional support:
Jack's constantly having to tell the Story recalls
humorous parallels in Huckleberry Finn; Speedy
Parker recalls Jim; the unlikely duo of Jack Sawyer and Richard Stoat and their equally incredible
adventures read like something out of Tom Sawyer's
imagination.

  Although both King and Straub have acknowledged the influence of Twain, Tolkien, Lewis, and
others on it, the novel transcends its sources.
It may be an encyclopedic treatment of science
fiction and the fantastic, yet it extends beyond
either, weaving intricate patterns of shifting
realities in which science fiction provides images
for fantasy, as when the smiling werewolf reminds
Jack of the creature in the film Alien (262).
Horror is both literal and figurative; Lori, the
waitress at Oatley's Tap, looks like a vampire,
for example, as does Morgan of Orris. Jack Sawyer's fictional aunt, Helen Vaughan, emerges from
the horror fiction of Arthur Machen. Mainstream
fiction appears in the guise of Sunlight Gardener
and Smokey Updike, who were named "with tongue
firmly in cheek" after John Gardener and John Updike, "two writers lionized by the critical establishment that has so often discounted horror and
fantasy fiction" (Winter, "Quest" 67).

  The alternate worlds of the novel are reciprocal. Burying an apple core in the Territories
can manifest in this world as an earthquake; a political assassination there results in World War
II here. Underground testing in Nevada results in
the Blasted Lands with their mutated horrors. And
the genres that blend to create The Talisman are
equally reciprocal, as King and Straub highlight
fantastic elements by endowing them with science-fictional rationale, and give science-fictional elements greater depth by allying them with
traditional fantasy. Even the fairy tale enters
into the novel at the level of metaphor and simile, as Jack recalls the door of a root cellar,
"set into a grassy mound like a door in a fairy

136

tale" (265).

Religion is also a strong element in the
novel, both as object of scrutiny (the false religion of Sunlight Gardener) and as image. When
Jack sets out on his quest, he parallels Christ in
Gethsemane; the cup cannot pass from him, however,
he accepts the quest, and ultimately becomes
Jason, a god-image in the Territories. Later, the
ironically named Sunlight Gardener urges Jack to
confess. In an inversion typical of King's strat-
egies in The Stand and The Eyes of the Dragon,
Gardener serves the Black force while dressed in
stainless white--he is the "White Man" to Wolf.
When he plays with a heavy key ring during Jack's
interrogation, he becomes a perverted Peter,
holding the keys to the nether kingdom, literally
guarding the entry to Gehenna.

Cancer remains a central threat--both the
physical cancer killing Lily Cavenaugh and the
figurative cancer afflicting our world and the
Territories. Politics enter in as well. Straub
refers to King's vision of "Reagan's America"
(cited in Winter, "Quest" 68), while references to
Nixon and Agnew reiterate the theme of corrupted
power. Sexuality likewise appears, but more as
potential homosexual assault than anything else.
Jack Sawyer's increasing physical beauty (coupled
with the absence of continuing female characters
except for the invalid Lily Cavenaugh and the
dying Queen of the Territories) makes his encounters with homosexuality inevitable. During the
episodes at the Sunlight Home, such references
increase, parallelling the boys' sublimated sexuality and providing an outlet for Gardener's
sadism.

On the deepest level, however, The Talisman
remains true to King's concerns from his earliest
works. Chaos intrudes upon order; the hero must
restore balance. To an extent, The Talisman reads
like anti-Carrie; Jack Sawyer accepts his powers,
wielding them responsibly and triumphing over
them. The struggle between Black and White central to The Stand, The Dark Tower, and The Eyes of
the Dragon continues to a more positive conclusion. In the beginning, Jack defines his quest in
terms of "NIGHT and DAY, MOON and SUN; DARK and
LIGHT" (25); at the end, a rainbow of light dis-
pels the darkness around Lily Cavenaugh, even as

the radiance of the talisman fades--another imagistic inversion. The novel ends with the victory
of the White force: in her white bedroom, the
Queen of the Territories opens her eyes.

 The Talisman repays a second reading. The
pace remains steady, but the narrative moves with
a quiet inexorability that makes Leerhsen's reference to "glacial" pacing inappropriate. It is
long; yet it requires length as it forces the
reader out of easy thought patterns and into tangential worlds where alternatives multiply until,
with Phil Sawyer, the reader realizes that there
may yet be Territories even beyond the Territories.

Chapter VIII

. . . AND BEYOND

In the September 6, 1985 issue of <u>Publishers</u>
<u>Weekly</u> Leonore Fleischer wrote:

> I got a postcard from one of my favorite
> people, a bestselling author, who de-
> manded, in a tone so plaintive it could
> be heard on a postcard, "Now I want to
> know about Stephen King's $10-million,
> two-book deal. Is it true?" Yes, J.,
> it's true . . . .

The books in question--<u>Misery</u> and <u>The Tommyknock-</u>
<u>ers</u>--will be the last of four to be published be-
tween September 1986 and November 1987, the first
two (already under contract) being <u>It</u> and the
trade edition of <u>The Eyes of the Dragon</u>. In light
of King's track record to date, these four are almost certain to be back-to-back bestsellers, but
they have generated interest beyond that single
fact.
     The decision to publish all four within just
over a year represents a major shift on the part
of publishers. After all, King resorted to the
Bachman pseudonym at least in part because of the
restriction placed on him not to publish more than
a single major work each year . . . and now he
plans on releasing four.
     In addition, the terms of the agreement are
unique. Although NAL receives paperback rights to
<u>Misery</u> and <u>The Tommyknockers</u>, the contract speci-
fies a fifteen-year expiration date for the hardcover rights going to Viking for <u>Misery</u> and to
Putnam for <u>The Tommyknockers</u> (Foltz). After that,
hardcover rights revert to Stephen King.
     Taken in conjunction with a record-breaking
press run for <u>The Talisman</u>; innovative pre-publi-
cation sales at reduced cost through B. Dalton's
nation-wide book chain; and at least three feature
films and several television productions based on

139

King's works and scheduled for release over the
next months, the contract for Misery and The Tommyknockers indicates that King is indeed, and will
probably continue to be, a publishing phenomenon.

The four novels promise to generate further
interest, and possibily further controversy.

It is King's magnum opus, a work "about kids.
It's like a gigantic overexposition from 'The
Body' from 'Different Seasons.' . . . 'It' has had
me obsessed for for years" (Brown, "Shining
Through"). A long novel even by King's standards,
It promises a full range of horror effects, in-
cluding "every monster you could think of" ("Ste-
phen King's Torrent of Horror").

Winter describes the first draft as over
eleven hundred pages long, a complex work told
from multiple perspectives and using two variant
narrative times, based loosely on a theme from
his earlier story, "The Boogeyman," that perhaps
the monsters we feared as children really existed;
in It belief in the creature is sufficient to give
the creature life. As is usual with King, the
novel is set in Maine; six characters return to
the town where they had lived as children, each
apparently impelled to discover exactly what happened to them in the sewer in Derry, Maine, in
1958. Roughly parallelling Straub's Floating
Dragon, the novel works from the thesis that "It"
is calling the characters together, forcing a
final confrontation (Art 153-155). As early as
1983, Straub noted that he and King seemed to be
"collaborating unconsciously already," since
"Steve's novel It and my novel Floating Dragon are
strangely parallel" ("King New Novel Advance").

Little more need be said of the next novel,
The Eyes of the Dragon, except to applaud King's
decision to give the work wider distribution than
it received as a limited edition. Unlike The Dark
Tower, Eyes is a complete work, strong enough to
stand against his other publications in spite of
its being intended originally for a juvenile audience.

The third novel, Misery, has been described
as "Sort of a realistic horrifying story of the
price paid by a novelist's fame . . . a dark
fantasy drawn from King's experience with fame and
popularity" (Winter, cited in "Stephen King's
Torrent of Horror"). Also a transitional novel,

it has more the sense of a Richard Bachman novel than the other three. In fact, King has intimated that had Thinner not forced him to acknowledge the pen-name, he would have published Misery as a Bachman; it has, he notes, "a Bachman feel to it" (Brown, "Shining Through").

The fourth, The Tommyknockers, examines our infatuation with gadgetry. Readers interested in a sneak preview have an unusual opportunity with The Tommyknockers, since "The Revelations of 'Becka Paulson," published in Rolling Stone (July 19/ August 2, 1984), is an excerpt from the novel. In that story, 'Becka Paulson runs afoul of a television set; she becomes so absorbed in it and its apparent revelations about her husband, her neighbors, and herself, that it destroys her and her husband (see SW 179-181). Elsewhere, King has referred to a passage he has been working on for some time, about a Coca-Cola vending machine that comes to life; from what he has said about The Tommyknockers, that might also be an episode from the novel.

Even this brief look at the forthcoming novels indicates that King is remaining true to the kind of fiction he does best while simultaneously stretching beyond what he has achieved to date. The novels seem almost assured to reach bestseller status; and with them coming so quickly, it seems equally possible that King might repeat his unique achievement in being the only American writer to have three books on the lists simultaneously.

Thus far, this series has concentrated on King as writer: the Bachman novels in Stephen King as Richard Bachman: the short stories in The Shorter Works of Stephen King; his novels in this volume. There is much more to King, however. A subsequent volume will examine the relationship between King and film: films made from his novels and stories; films produced from King's scripts or directed by King; even a brief look at King as actor. Another will consider King as social critic, literary critic, and cultural phenomenon, continuing what was begun here . . . an assessment of the many facets of Stephen King.

CHECKLIST OF WORKS BY AND ABOUT STEPHEN KING

This checklist is based on bibliographic studies by Stephanie Leonard (CR), Douglas Winter (Art), Marty Ketchum, Daniel J. H. Levack, and Jeff Levin (FI), and Marshall Tymn (DSK); on materials provided by other collectors and King enthusiasts, especially Barbara Bolan of Second Edition Books, Ted Dikty of Starmont House, Dan Klamkin of DMK Books, and Sandy Parigan; and on my own research.

Primary Bibliography

I. BOOK-LENGTH FICTION

Carrie. Garden City NY: Doubleday, 1974 [hardcover]; New York: NAL/Signet, 1976 [paperback].
Christine. West Kingston RI: Donald M. Grant, 1983 [limited edition]; New York: Viking, 1983 [hardcover]; New York: NAL/Signet, 1984 [paperback].
Cujo. New York: Mysterious Press, 1981 [limited edition]; New York: Viking, 1981 [hardcover]; New York: NAL/Signet, 1982 [paperback].
Cycle of the Werewolf. Westland MI: Land of Enchantment, 1983 [limited edition]; New York: NAL/Signet, 1985 [trade paperback]. Illustrated by Bernie Wrightson.
The Dead Zone. New York: Viking, 1979 [hardcover]; New York: NAL/Signet, 1980 [paperback].
The Eyes of the Dragon. Bangor ME: Philtrum, 1984 [limited edition]; trade edition scheduled for 1986-87.
Firestarter. Huntington Woods MI: Phantasia Press, 1980 [limited edition]; New York: Viking, 1980 [hardcover]; New York NAL/ Signet, 1981 [paperback].
The Long Walk. New York: NAL, 1979 [paperback].
Pet Sematary. Garden City NY: Doubleday, 1983 [hardcover]; New York: NAL/Signet, 1984 [paperback].
Rage (Richard Bachman). New York: NAL, 1977 [paperback].
Roadwork (Richard Bachman). New York: NAL, 1981 [paperback].
The Running Man (Richard Bachman). New York: NAL, 1982 [paperback].

'Salem's Lot. Garden City NY: Doubleday, 1975 [hardcover]; New York: NAL/Signet, 1976 [paperback].

The Shining. Garden City NY: Doubleday, 1977 [hardcover]; New York: NAL/Signet, 1978 [paperback].

The Stand. Garden City NY: Doubleday, 1978 [hardcover]; New York: NAL/Signet, 1979 [paperback].

The Talisman (with Peter Straub). West Kingston RI: Donald M. Grant, 1984 [limited edition]; New York: Viking and Putnam, 1984 [hardcover]: New York: Berkley, 1985 [paperback].

Thinner (Richard Bachman). New York: NAL, 1984 [hardcover].

Scheduled for publication:

It. New York: Viking, 1986-1987 [hardcover]; New York: NAL [paperback].

Misery. New York: Viking, 1987 [hardcover]; New York: NAL [paperback].

The Tommyknockers. New York: Putnam, 1987 [hardcover]; New York: NAL [paperback].

Unpublished manuscripts:

Sword in the Darkness (also referred to as Babylon Here)
Blaze
The Corner (incomplete)
Milkman (incomplete)
Welcome to Clearwater (incomplete)

In various interviews and studies, two other works are also mentioned: The Cannibals, a completed novel (FI 268); and 'Salem's Lot II, a sequel to SL King has discussed several times as a possible future project.

II. COLLECTIONS

The Bachman Books: Four Early Novels by Stephen King. New York: NAL, 1985 [hardcover]; NAL/Plume, October 1985 [paperback].
Includes:
Introduction: "Why I Was Richard Bachman"
Rage
The Long Walk
Roadwork
The Running Man

Creepshow. New York: NAL/Plume, 1982 [paperback]. Comic book adaptation; artwork by Bernie Wrightson.
Includes:
"Father´s Day"
"The Lonesome Death of Jordy Verrill"
"The Crate"
"Something to Tide You Over"
"They´re Creeping Up on You"

The Dark Tower: The Gunslinger. West Kingston RI: Donald M. Grant, 1982 [limited edition]. Illustrated by Michael Whelan.
Includes:
"The Gunslinger"
"The Way Station"
"The Oracle and the Mountains"
"The Slow Mutants"
"The Gunslinger and the Dark Man"
"Afterword"

Different Seasons. New York: Viking, 1982 [hardcover]; New York: NAL/Signet, 1983 [paperback].
Includes:
"Rita Hayworth and Shawshank Redemption"
"Apt Pupil"
"The Body"
"The Breathing Method"
"Afterword"

Night Shift. Garden City NY: Doubleday, 1978 [hardcover]; New York: NAL/Signet, 1979 [paperback].
Includes:
"Introduction," by John D. MacDonald
"Foreword"

144

"Jerusalem's Lot"
"Graveyard Shift"
"Night Surf"
"I Am the Doorway"
"The Mangler"
"The Boogeyman"
"Gray Matter"
"Battleground"
"Trucks"
"Sometimes They Come Back"
"Strawberry Spring"
"The Ledge"
"The Lawnmower Man"
"Quitters, Inc."
"I Know What You Need"
"Children of the Corn"
"The Last Rung on the Ladder"
"The Man Who Loved Flowers"
"One for the Road"
"The Woman in the Room"

Readings from Night Shift are available on Walden Tapes, including "Strawberry Spring," "The Boogeyman," "Graveyard Shift," "The Man Who Loved Flowers," "One for the Road," "The Last Rung on the Ladder," "I Know What You Need," "Jerusalem's Lot," and "I Am the Doorway." Stuart Leigh, Director. Warner Audio, 1985. $34.95 for six tapes.

Skeleton Crew. New York: Viking, 1985 [hardcover]; Santa Cruz CA: Scream Press [limited edition].
   Includes:
   "Introduction"
   "The Mist"
   "Here There Be Tygers"
   "The Monkey"
   "Cain Rose Up"
   "Mrs. Todd's Shortcut"
   "The Jaunt"
   "The Wedding Gig"
   "Paranoid: A Chant" (poem)
   "The Raft"
   "Word Processor of the Gods"
   "The Man Who Would Not Shake Hands"
   "Beachworld"
   "The Reaper's Image"

145

"Nona"
"For Owen" (poem)
"Survivor Type"
"Uncle Otto´s Truck"
"Morning Deliveries (Milkman #1)"
"Big Wheels: A Tale of the Laundry Game
    (Milkman #2)"
"Gramma"
"The Ballad of the Flexible Bullet"
"The Reach"
"Notes"

The Scream Press limited edition will also
include "The Revelations of ´Becka Paulson," a
fragment of a novel, The Tommyknockers, scheduled for publication in 1986-87.

Stephen King. New York: William Heinemann, Inc.
and Octopus Books, 1981 [hardcover].
    Includes:
    The Shining
    ´Salem´s Lot
    Night Shift
    Carrie

III. SHORT FICTION AND POETRY

"Apt Pupil: Summer of Corruption." <u>DS</u>, 1982.
"The Ballad of the Flexible Bullet." <u>The Magazine of Fantasy and Science Fiction</u>, June 1984; <u>SC</u>, 1985.
"Battleground." <u>Cavalier</u>, September 1972; <u>NS</u>, 1978.
"Beachworld." <u>Weird Tales</u>, 1985; <u>SC</u>, 1985.
"Before the Play." <u>Whispers</u>, August 1982.
"Big Wheels: A Tale of the Laundry Game." <u>New Terrors, 2</u>, ed. Ramsey Campbell (London: Pan, 1980); <u>New Terrors</u>, ed. Ramsey Campbell (New York: Pocket Books, 1982); <u>SC</u>, 1985.
"The Bird and the Album." <u>A Fantasy Reader: The Seventh World Fantasy Convention Program Book</u>, eds. Jeff Frane and Jack Rems (Berkeley, CA: The Seventh World Fantasy Convention, 1981). Excerpt from <u>It</u>.
"The Blue Air Compressor." <u>Onan</u>, January 1971; <u>Heavy Metal</u>, July 1981.
"The Body: Fall from Innocence." <u>DS</u>, 1982. Incorporates "Stud City" and "The Revenge of Lard Ass Hogan."
"The Boogeyman." <u>Cavalier</u>, March 1973; <u>Gent</u>, December 1975: <u>NS</u>, 1978.
"The Breathing Method: A Winter's Tale." <u>DS</u>, 1982.
"Cain Rose Up". <u>Ubris</u>, Spring 1968; <u>SC</u>, 1985.
"The Cat from Hell." <u>Cavalier</u>, June 1977; <u>Tales of Unknown Horror</u>, ed. Peter Haining (London: New English Library, 1978); <u>The Year's Finest Fantasy</u>, ed. Terry Carr (New York: Putnam, 1978; New York: Berkley, 1979); <u>Magicats!</u>, eds. Jack Dann and Gardner Dozois (New York: Ace, 1984); <u>New Bern Magazine</u>, March-April 1984; Top Horror, ed. Josh Pachter (Munich, West Germany: Wilhelm Heyne Verlag).
"Children of the Corn." <u>Penthouse</u>, March 1977; <u>NS</u>, 1978; <u>Cults! An Anthology of Secret Societies, Sects, and the Supernatural</u>, eds. Martin H. Greenberg and Charles C. Waugh (New York: Beaufort, 1983).
"The Crate." <u>Gallery</u>, July 1979; <u>Fantasy Annual III</u>, ed. Terry Carr (New York: Pocket, 1981); <u>The Arbor House Treasury of Horror and the Supernatural</u>, comps. Bill Pronzini, Barry N. Malzberg, and Martin H. Greenberg (New York: Arbor House, 1981); <u>Creepshow</u>, 1982.

147

"Crouch End." New Tales of the Cthulhu Mythos, ed. Ramsey Campbell (Sauk City, WI: Arkham House, 1980).

"Cujo." Science Fiction Digest, January/February 1982 (excerpt from Cujo).

"Cycle of the Werewolf." Heavy Metal, December 1983 (excerpt from Cycle of the Werewolf).

"The Dark Man." Ubris, Spring 1969 (poem).

"Do the Dead Sing?" Yankee, November 1981; as "The Reach," SC, 1985.

"Dolan's Cadillac." Castle Rock, February through June 1985.

"The Fifth Quarter" (John Swithen). Cavalier, April 1972.

"Firestarter." Omni, July-August 1980 (excerpts from Firestarter).

"For Owen." SC, 1985 (poem).

"The Glass Floor." Startling Mystery Stories, Fall 1967.

"Gramma." Weirdbook, Spring 1984; SC, 1985.

"Graveyard Shift." Cavalier, October 1970; NS, 1978; The 21st Pan Book of Horror Stories, ed. Herbert Van Thal (London: Pan, 1980).

"Gray Matter." Cavalier, October 1973; NS, 1978; The Arbor House Necropolis, ed. Bill Pronzini (New York: Arbor House, 1981; New York: Priam, 1981).

"The Gunslinger." The Magazine of Fantasy and Science Fiction, October 1978; The Year's Finest Fantasy, Volume Two, ed. Terry Carr (New York: Berkley, 1980); DT, 1982.

"The Gunslinger and the Dark Man." The Magazine of Fantasy and Science Fiction, November 1981; DT, 1982.

"Harrison State Park '68." Ubris, Fall 1968 (poem).

"Here There Be Tygers." Ubris, Spring 1968; SC, 1985.

"I Am the Doorway." Cavalier, March 1971; NS, 1978.

"I Know What You Need." Cosmopolitan, September 1976; NS, 1978; Isaac Asimov's Magical World of Fantasy (New York: Signet, 1985).

"I Was a Teenage Grave Robber." Comics Review, 1965; as "In a Half-World of Terror," Stories of Suspense 1966.

"In a Half-World of Terror." Reprint title for "I Was a Teenage Grave Robber."

"It Grows on You." Marshroots, 1975; Whispers, August 1982; Death, ed. Stuart David Schiff (New York: Playboy, 1982).

"The Jaunt." Twilight Zone Magazine, April 1981; Gallery, December 1981; Great Stories from Twilight Zone Magazine, September 1982; SC, 1985.

"Jerusalem's Lot." NS, 1978; The World Fantasy Awards, Volume Two, eds. Stuart David Schiff and Fritz Leiber (Garden City, NY: Doubleday, 1980).

"The Last Rung on the Ladder." NS, 1978.

"The Lawnmower Man." Cavalier, May 1975; NS, 1978; Bizarre Adventures, December 1981 (comic book adaptation).

"The Ledge." Penthouse, July 1976; NS, 1978.

"The Lonesome Death of Jordy Verrill." Retitling of "Weeds" for Creepshow, 1982.

"The Man Who Loved Flowers." Gallery, August 1977; NS, 1978.

"The Man Who Would Not Shake Hands." Shadows 4, ed. Charles L. Grant (Garden City NY: Doubleday 1981, 1985); Fantasy Annual V, ed. Terry Carr (New York: Pocket, 1982); SC, 1985.

"Man With a Belly." Cavalier, December 1978; Gent, November/December 1979.

"The Mangler." Cavalier, December 1972; NS, 1978; The 21st Pan Book of Horror Stories, ed. Herbert Van Thal (London: Pan, 1980); The Arbor House Celebrity Book of Horror Stories, eds. Martin H. Greenberg and Charles Waugh (New York: Arbor House, 1982; New York: Priam, 1982).

"The Mist." Dark Forces, ed. Kirby McCauley (New York: Viking, 1980; New York: Bantam, 1981); SC, 1985.

"The Monkey." Gallery, November 1980; Fantasy Annual IV, ed. Terry Carr (New York: Pocket, 1981); Horrors, ed. Charles L. Grant (New York: Playboy, 1981); Modern Masters of Horror, ed. Frank Coffey (New York: Coward, McCann & Geoghegan, 1981; New York: Ace, 1982); The Year's Best Horror Stories Series IX, ed. Karl Edward Wagner (New York: DAW, 1981); SC, 1985.

"The Monster in the Closet." Ladies' Home Journal, October 1981 (excerpt from Cujo).

"Morning Deliveries (Milkman #1)." SC, 1985.

"Mrs. Todd's Shortcut." <u>Redbook</u>, May 1984: <u>SC</u>, 1985.
"The Night of the Tiger." <u>The Magazine of Fantasy and Science Fiction</u>, February 1978; <u>More Tales of Unknown Horror</u>, ed. Peter Haining (London: New English Library, 1979); <u>The Year's Best Horror Stories Series VII</u>, ed. Gerald W. Page (New York: DAW, 1979; <u>Chamber of Horrors</u> (London: Octopus, 1984).
"Night Surf." <u>Ubris</u>, Spring 1969; <u>Cavalier</u>, August 1974; <u>NS</u>, 1978.
"Nona." <u>Shadows</u>, ed. Charles L. Grant (Garden City NY: Doubleday, 1978; New York: Playboy, 1980); <u>The Dodd, Mead Gallery of Horror</u>, ed. Charles L. Grant (New York: Dodd, Mead, 1983); <u>SC</u>, 1985.
"One for the Road." <u>Maine</u>, March/April 1977; <u>NS</u>, 1978.
"The Oracle and the Mountains." <u>The Magazine of Fantasy and Science Fiction</u>, February 1981; <u>DT</u>, 1982.
"Paranoid: A Chant." <u>SC</u>, 1985 (poem).
"The Plant." Self-published, 1982, 1983.
"Quitters, Inc." <u>NS</u>, 1978; <u>Best Detective Stories of the Year</u>, ed. Edward D. Hoch (New York: Dutton, 1979); <u>The Science Fiction WeightLoss Book</u>, eds. Isaac Asimov, George R. R. Martin, and Martin H. Greenberg (New York: Crown, 1983).
"The Raft." <u>Gallery</u>, November 1982; <u>Twilight Zone Magazine</u>, May/June 1983; <u>SC</u>, 1985.
"The Reach." ("Do the Dead Sing?"); <u>SC</u>, 1985.
"The Reaper's Image." <u>Startling Mystery Stories</u>, Spring 1969; <u>The 17th Fontana Book of Great Ghost Stories</u>, ed. R. Chetwynd-Hayes (London: Fontana, 1981); <u>SC</u>, 1985.
"The Return of Timmy Baterman." <u>Satyricon II Program Book</u>, ed. Rusty Burke (Knoxville, TN: Satyricon II/DeepSouthCon XXI, 1983). Excerpt from <u>Pet Sematary</u>.
"The Revelations of 'Becka Paulson." <u>Rolling Stone</u>, July 19/August 2, 1984. Excerpt from <u>The Tommyknockers</u>. Included in the Scream Press limited edition of <u>Skeleton Crew</u>.
"The Revenge of Lard Ass Hogan." <u>The Maine Review</u>, July 1975; incorporated into "The Body," <u>DS</u>, 1982.
"Rita Hayworth and Shawshank Redemption: Hope

Springs Eternal." DS, 1982.
"The Shining." Ramada Reflections, June 1977 (excerpt from The Shining).
"Skybar." The Do-It-Yourself Bestseller, eds. Tom Silberkleit and Jerry Biederman (New York: Doubleday, Dolphin 1982).
"Slade." The Maine Campus, June-August 1970.
"The Slow Mutants." The Magazine of Fantasy and Science Fiction, July 1981; DT, 1982.
"Sometimes They Come Back." Cavalier, March 1974; NS, 1978.
"Squad D." Unpublished; accepted for The Last Dangerous Visions, ed. Harlan Ellison.
"The Star Invaders." Self-published; Durham, ME: Triad, Inc. and Gaslight Books, 1964.
"Strawberry Spring." Ubris, Fall 1968; Cavalier, November 1975; Gent, February 1977; NS, 1978; An International Treasury of Mystery and Suspense, ed. Marie R. Reno (New York: Doubleday, 1983).
"Stud City." Ubris, Fall 1969; incorporated into "The Body," DS, 1982.
"Suffer the Little Children." Cavalier, February 1972; Nightmares, ed. Charles L. Grant (New York: Playboy, 1979); The Evil Image: Two Centuries of Gothic Short Fiction and Poetry, eds. Patricia L. Skarda and Nora Crow Jaffe (New York: New American Library, Meridian, 1981); 65 Great Spine Chillers, ed. Mary Danby (New York: London: Octopus, 1982).
"Survivor Type." Terrors, ed. Charles L. Grant (New York: Playboy, 1982); SC, 1985.
"Trucks." Cavalier, June 1973: NS, 1978.
"Uncle Otto's Truck." Yankee, October 1983; The Year's Best Horror Stories Series XII, ed. Karl Edward Wagner (New York: DAW, 1984).
"Untitled Poem." Onan, 1971.
"The Way Station." The Magazine of Fantasy and Science Fiction, April 1980; DT, 1982.
"The Wedding Gig." Ellery Queen's Mystery Magazine, December 1, 1980; SC, 1985.
"Weeds." Cavalier, May 1976; Nugget, April 1979; as "The Lonesome Death of Jordy Verrill," Creepshow, 1982.
"The Woman in the Room." NS, 1978.
"The Word Processor." Playboy, January 1983; as "Word Processor of the Gods," SC, 1985.

IV. SELECTED NON-FICTION AND CRITICISM BY KING

1. Book-length criticism:

Danse Macabre. New York: Everest House, 1981
[limited and trade hardcover]; New York:
Berkley, 1982 [paperback].

2. Articles, reviews, and other non-fiction:

"Afterword." DT, 1982.
"Afterword." DS, 1982.
"Afterword." Firestarter, 1982 [paperback].
"Black Magic and Music." Bangor Historical Soci-
ety, 1983. Concert program.
"Between Rock and a Soft Place." Playboy (January
1982).
"Books." Adelina (June-November 1980). Review
column, with discussions of:
Burnt Offerings by Robert Marasco (June 1980)
The Brave and the Free by Leslie Waller (June
1980; July 1980)
Mayday by Thomas M. Block (August 1980)
Cold Moon Over Babylon by Michael McDowell
(August 1980)
No Name by Wilkie Collins (November 1980).
"The Cannibal and the Cop." Washington Post Book
World, 1 November 1981; Shadowings. Ed. Doug-
las E. Winter. Mercer Island WA: Starmont
House, 1983.
"Cat from Hell." Castle Rock: The Stephen King
Newsletter (June 1985). Discussion of how King
wrote "The Cat from Hell."
"The Collected Stories of Ray Bradbury." Chicago
Tribune Bookworld, 10 October 1980.
"Danse Macabre." Book Digest (September 1981).
Condensed version.
"Digging the Boogens." Twilight Zone Magazine
(July 1982).
"Dr. Seuss and the Two Faces of Fantasy." Pre-
sented to the International Conference on the
Fantastic in the Arts, 24 March 1984; Fantasy
Review, No. 68 (June 1984).
"The Doll Who Ate His Mother." Whispers, No.
11/12 (October 1978).
"Don´t Be Cruel." TV Guide, 30 April-6 May 1983.
Letter to editor.
"The Evil Dead." Twilight Zone Magazine (November

1982).

"Favorite Films." Washington Post, 24 Juune 1982.

"Foreword." NS, 1978.

"Foreword." In Stalking the Nightmare. By Harlan Ellison. Huntington Woods MI: Phantasia Press, 1982 [limited edition]; New York: Berkley, 1984 [paperback].

"Foreword." In Tales from the Nightside. Ed. Charles L. Grant. Sauk City WI: Arkham House, 1981 [hardcover].

"The Fright Report." Oui (January 1978).

"Garbage Truck." See "King´s Garbage Truck."

"Guilty Pleasures." Film Comment (May/June 1981).

"The Horror Market Writer and the Ten Bears." Writer´s Digest (November 1973).

"Horrors!" Games (October 1983). Crossword puzzle with clues by King.

"Horrors!" TV Guide, 30 October-5 November 1982.

"The Horrors of ´79." Rolling Stone, 27 December 1979-10 January 1980.

"How to Scare a Woman to Death." In Murderess Ink. Ed. Dilys Winn. New York: Bell, 1979 [hardcover]; New York: Bell, 1980 [paperback].

"Imagery and the Third Eye." The Writer (October 1980); Maine Alumnus (December 1981); The Writer´s Handbook. Ed. Sylvia K. Burack. Boston MA: The Writer, Inc., 1984.

"Introduction." The Arbor House Treasury of Horror and the Supernatural. Comps. Bill Pronzini, Barry Malzberg, and Martin H. Greenberg. New York: Arbor House, 1981 [hardcover]; New York: Arbor House/Priam, 1981 [paperback].

"Introduction." The Blackboard Jungle. By Evan Hunter. New York: Arbor House, Library of Contemporary Americana, 1984 [paperback].

"Introduction." Frankenstein/ Dracula/ Dr. Jekyl and Mr. Hyde. By Mary Shelley, Bram Stoker, and Robert Louis Stevenson. New York: NAL/Signet, 1978 [paperback].

"Introduction." The Shapes of Midnight. By Joseph Payne. New York: Berkley, 1980 [paperback].

"Introduction." Tales by Moonlight. Ed. Jessica Salmonson. Chicago IL: Robert Garcia, 1983 [hardcover]; New York: Tor, 1984 [paperback].

"Introduction." When Michael Calls. By John Farris. New York: Pocket Books 1981 [paperback].

"Introduction: The Importance of Being Forry." Mr. Monster´s Movie Gold. By Forrest J. Ackerman.

153

Virginia Beach/Norfolk VA: Donning, 1982 [paperback].

"Introduction to the Marvel Edition of **Franken-stein**." Frankenstein, or The Modern Prometheus. By Mary Shelley. New York: Dodd Mead, 1983 [limited edition, hardcover, paperback].

"The Irish King." New York Daily News, 16 March 1984.

"King's Garbage Truck." The Maine Campus, 20 February 1969-21 May 1970. Weekly column.

Letter. Fantasy Review (January 1984): 45. Discussion of anthologies and reprint publishing.

Letter. Fantasy Review (May 1985): 11. Repudiation of hoax-review (Love Lessons).

Letter. TV Guide. 30 April-6 May 1983. Elvis Presley and rock 'n' roll.

"Lists That Matter (Number 7)." Castle Rock: The Stephen King Newsletter (August 1985). List of King's ten favorite films.

"Lists That Matter (Number 8)." Castle Rock: The Stephen King Newsletter (September 1985). List of ten worst movies of all time.

"The Ludlum Attraction." Washington Post Book World, 7 March 1982. Review of The Parsifal Mosaic.

"Market Writer and the Ten Bears." Writer's Digest (November 1983).

"Mentors." Rolling Stone College Papers, 15 April 1982.

"A Message from Stephen King to Waldenbooks People." Waldenbooks Booknotes (August 1983).

"My First Car." Gentlemen's Quarterly (July 1984). Brief mention of Cujo and Christine.

"My High School Horrors." Sourcebook: The Magazine for Seniors, 1982.

"1984, a Bad Year If you Fear Friday the 13th." New York Times, 12 April 1984.

"Not Guilty." New York Times Book Review, 24 October 1976.

"Notes on Horror." Quest (June 1982). Excerpts from Danse Macabre.

"On Becoming a Brand Name." Adelina (February 1980); Fear Itself: The Horror Fiction of Stephen King. Eds. Tim Underwood and Chuck Miller. San Francisco CA/Columbia PA: Underwood-Miller, 1982 [limited edition and hardcover]; New York: NAL/Plume, 1984 [paperback].

"On The Shining and Other Perpetrations." Whispers, No. 17/188 (August 1982).

"Peter Straub: An Informal Appreciation." World Fantasy Convention ´82. Ed. Kennedy Poyser. New Haven CT: The Eighth World Fantasy Convention, 1982.

"A Pilgrim´s Progress." American Bookseller (January 1980).

"The Politics of Limited Editions." Castle Rock: The Stephen King Newsletter (June-July 1985).

"A Profile of Robert Bloch." World Fantasy Convention 1983. Ed. Robert Weinberg. Oak Forest IL: Weird Tales Ltd., 1983.

"Ross Thomas Stirs the Pot." Washington Post Book World, 16 October 1983. Review of Missionary Stew.

"The Sorry State of TV Shows." TV Guide, 5 December 1981. Excerpt from Danse Macabre.

"Scare Movies." Cosmopolitan (April 1981).

"Special Make-Up Effects and the Writer." Grande Illusions. By Tom Savini. Pittsburgh PA: Imagine, Inc., 1983 [paperback]; reprinted as Bizarro. New York: Crown, 1983 [paperback].

"Stephen King." A Gift from Maine. By Maine´s Foremost Artists and Writers and James Plummer´s Sixth Grade Class. Portland ME: Gannet, 1983. Biographical sketch.

"Stephen King´s 10 Favorite Horror Books or Short Stories." The Book of Lists #3. Comps. Amy Wallace, David Wallechinsky, and Irving Wallace. New York: William Morrow, 1983 [paperback].

Untitled. Dreamworks (Summer 1981). Description of a recurring dream.

"Visit with an Endangered Species." Playboy (January 1982).

"What Went Down When Magyk Went Up." New York Times Book Review 10 February 1985. Review of Glitz, by Elmore Leonard.

"When Is TV Too Scary for Children?" TV Guide, 13-19 June 1981.

"Why I Am for Gary Hart." The New Republic, 4 June 1984.

"Why We Crave Horror Movies." Playboy (January 1981).

"Writing a First Novel." The Writer (June 1875).

"The Writing Life: An Interview with Myself." Writer´s Digest (January 1979).

"You Gotta Put on the Gruesome Mask and Go Booga-Booga." TV Guide, 5-11 December 1981.

V. FILM VERSIONS OF KING´S FICTION

The Boogeyman. Tantalus, 1984.
Jeffrey C. Schiro, producer.
Jeffrey C. Schiro, director.
Jeffrey C. Schiro, screenwriter.
Cast: Michael Reid, Bert Linden.

Carrie. United Artists, 1976.
Paul Monash, producer.
Brian de Palma, director.
Lawrence D. Cohen, screenwriter.
Cast: Sissy Spacek, Piper Laurie, Amy Irving,
William Katt, Nancy Allen, John Travolta.

Cat´s Eye. MGM/United Artists, 1984.
Dino de Laurentiis, executive producer.
Martha Schumacher, producer.
Lewis Teague, director.
Stephen King, screenwriter.
Cast: Drew Barrymore, Candy Clark, Joe Cortese,
Robert Hayes, Alan King, Patti LuPone, Kenneth
McMillan, James Wood.

Children of the Corn. New World Pictures, 1984.
Donald P. Borchers and Terrence Kirby, pro-
ducers.
Earl Glick and Charles K. Weber, executive pro-
ducers.
Fritz Kiersch, director.
George Goldsmith, screenwriter.
Cast: Peter Horton, Linda Hamilton, R. G. Arm-
strong, John Franklin, Courtney Gains, Robby
Kiger, AnneMarie McEvoy, Julie Maddalena.

Christine. Columbia Pictures, 1983.
Richard Kobritz, producer.
Kirby McCauley and Mark Tarlov, executive pro-
ducers.
John Carpenter, director.
Bill Phillips, screenwriter.
Cast: Keith Gordon, John Stockwell, Alexandra
Paul, Robert Prosky, Harry Dean Stanton.

Creepshow. Warner Brothers, 1982.
Richard P. Rubenstein, producer.
George A. Romero, director.
Stephen King, screenwriter.

Cast: Adrienne Barbeau, Hal Holbrook, Viveca Lindfors, E. G. Marshall, Leslie Nielsen, Carrie Nye, Fritz Weaver, Ted Danson, Robert Harper, Ed Harris, Don Keefer. Jon Lormer, Elizabeth Regan, Gaylen Ross, Warner Shook.

Cujo. Warner Brothers, 1983.
    Daniel H. Blatt and Robert Singer, producers.
    Lewis Teague, director.
    Don Carlos Dunaway and Lauren Currier, screen-
        writers.
    Cast: Dee Wallace, Danny Pintauro, Daniel Hugh-
    Kelly, Christopher Stone, Ed Lauter, Kaiulani
    Lee, Mills Watson.

The Dead Zone. Paramount Pictures, 1983.
    Debra Hill, producer.
    Kirby McCauley, executive producer.
    David Cronenberg, director.
    Jeffrey Boam, screenwriter.
    Cast: Christopher Walken, Brooke Adams, Tom
    Skerrit, Herbert Lom, Martin Sheen, Anthony
    Zerbe, Colleen Dewhurst, Nicholas Campbell.

Firestarter. Universal Pictures, 1984.
    Frank Capra, Jr., producer.
    Mark Lester, Director.
    Stanley Mann, screenwriter.
    Cast: David Keith, Drew Barrymore, Freddie
    Jones, Heather Lockyear, Martin Sheen, George
    C. Scott, Art Carney, Louise Fletcher, Moses
    Gunn.

´Salem´s Lot. Warner Brothers, 1979 (television
    mini-series).
    Richard Kobritz, producer.
    Tobe Hooper, director.
    Paul Monash, screenwriter.
    Cast: David Soul, James Mason, Lance Kerwin,
    Bonnie Bedelia, Lew Ayres, Julie Cobb.

The Shining. Warner Brothers, 1980.
    Stanley Kubrick, producer.
    Stanley Kubrick, director.
    Stanley Kubrick and Diane Johnson, screen-
        writers.
    Cast: Jack Nicholson, Shelley Duvall, Danny
    Lloyd, Scatman Crothers, Barry Nelson, Joe

Turkel.

The Woman in the Room. Darkwoods, 1984.
Gregory Melton, producer.
Douglas Venturelli, executive producer.
Frank Darabont, director.
Frank Darabont, screenwriter.
<u>Cast</u>: Michael Cornelison, Dee Croxton, Brian
Libby

The Word Processor. Laurel Productions (George A.
Romero and Richard Rubenstein), for <u>Tales from
the Darkside</u> television series, 1984.
Richard Rubenstein, executive producer.
David E. Vogel, producer.
Michael Gornick, director.
<u>Cast</u>: Bruce Davison

Films in Production

Silver Bullet. Based on <u>Cycle of the Werewolf</u>.
North Carolina Film Corporation (Dino de
Laurentiis). Scheduled release date: October
1985.
Martha Schumacher, producer.
Dan Attias, director.
Stephen King, screenwriter.
<u>Cast</u>: Corey Haim, Everett Mcgill, Gary
Busey.

Maximum Overdrive. Based on "Trucks" (<u>NS</u>).
North Carolina Film Corporation (Dino de
Laurentiis).
Dino de Laurentiis, producer.
Stephen King, director.
Stephen King, screenwriter.
<u>Cast</u>: Emilio Estevez, Pat Hingle.

The Body. Based on "The Body" (<u>DS</u>). Scheduled
to begin filming July 1985.
Rob Reiner, director.

Gramma. Teleplay by Harlan Ellison. Scheduled
for <u>The Twilight Zone</u>, CBS television, 1985.
William Friedkin, director.
Cast: Barret Oliver.

The Running Man. Scheduled to begin filming in

158

October, 1985, in Edmonton, Alberta, Canada.
George Cosmatos, director (<u>Rambo</u>)
Cast: Christopher Reeve

Pet Sematary. Screenplay by Stephen King.
With George A. Romero. Filming site: Maine.
Scheduled to begin production, March 1986.
Richard Rubenstein, producer.
George A. Romero, director.

The Stand. Screenplay by Stephen King. With
George A. Romero. An early draft called for
a two-part film: <u>The Stand, I</u> would deal
with the flu epidemic; <u>The Stand, II</u>, with
the struggle against the Dark Man. The
third draft incorporates both into a three-
hour film. Filming site: Texas.

The Talisman. Optioned by Stephen Spielberg.

The Long Walk.

King's screenplays (not produced)

<u>Battleground</u>
<u>Children of the Corn</u>
<u>Cujo</u>
<u>The Dead Zone</u>
<u>Night Shift</u>
<u>The Shotgunners</u>
<u>The Shining</u>
<u>Something Wicked This Way Comes</u> (Bradbury)

King has been involved in a number of other film
possibilities:
   <u>Creepshow II</u>, a sequel to <u>Creepshow</u>. The project is critical if not dead.
   Martin Poll Productions optioned "Battleground," "Strawberry Spring," and "I Know What You
Need" for an NBC-TV anthology. The project died.
   Milton Subotsky optioned "The Lawnmower Man,"
"Trucks," and "The Mangler" for an anthology film,
plus rights to "The Ledge," "Quitters, Inc.," and
"Sometimes They Come Back." King arranged with
Subotsky for rights to produce <u>Cat's Eye</u>. King
has said that every story in <u>NS</u> except "Jeru-
salem's Lot" has been discussed as a film.

Secondary Bibliography

VI. SELECTED CRITICISM AND REVIEWS

1. Full-length studies of King's works:

Collings, Michael R. The Films of Stephen King.
    Mercer Island WA: Starmont House, (in
    progress).
--------- The Many Facets of Stephen King. Mer-
    cer Island WA: Starmont House, 1985.
--------- Stephen King as Richard Bachman. Mer-
    cer Island WA: Starmont House, 1985.
--------- The Stephen King Concordance. Mercer
    Island WA: Starmont House, (in progress).
--------- The Stephen King Phenomenon. Mercer
    Island WA: Starmont House, (in progress).
Collings, Michael R. and David A. Engebretson.
    The Shorter Works of Stephen King. Mercer
    Island WA: Starmont House, 1985.
Schweitzer, Darrell, ed. Discovering Stephen King.
    Mercer Island WA: Starmont House, 1985.
        Ben P. Indick, "What Makes Him So Scary."
        Alan Warren, "Has Success Spoiled Stephen
            King?"
        Don Herron, "The Biggest Horror Fan of Them
            All."
        Gary William Crawford, "Stephen King's Amer-
            ican Gothic."
        Chet Williamson, "The Early Tales: Stephen
            King and Startling Mystery Stories."
        Bernadette Bosky, "Stephen King and Peter
            Straub: Fear and Friendship."
        Michael R. Collings, "The Stand: Science
            Fiction into Fantasy."
        Debra Stump, "Stephen King With a Twist: The
            E.C. Influence."
        Randall D. Larson, "Cycle of the Werewolf
            and the Moral Tradition."
        Robert M. Price. "Stephen King and the
            Lovecraft Mythos."
        Don D'Ammassa, "Three by Bachman."
        Debra Stump, "A Matter of Choice: King's
            Cujo and Malamud's The Natural."
        Leonard G. Heldreth. "The Ultimate Horror:
            The Dead Child in Stephen King's Stories
            and Novels." .

160

     Darrell Schweitzer, "Collecting Stephen
       King."
     Sanford Z. Meschkow, "Synopses of Stephen
       King's Fiction."
     Marshall B. Tymn, "Stephen King: A Biblio-
       graphy."
Underwood, Tim and Chuck Miller, eds. Fear Itself:
The Horror Fiction of Stephen King. San Francisco CA: Underwood-Miller, 1982 [limited,
hardcover]; New York: NAL/Plume, 1984 [paper-
back].
     Peter Straub, "Meeting Stevie."
     Stephen King, "On Becoming a Brand Name."
     Burton Hatlen, "Beyond the Kittery Bridge:
       Stephen King's Maine."
     Chelsea Quinn Yarbro, "Cinderella's Re-
       venge--Twists on Fairy Tale and Mythic
       Themes in the Work of Stephen King."
     Don Herron, "Horror Springs in the Fiction
       of Stephen King."
     Fritz Leiber, "Horror Hits a High."
     Bill Warren, "The Movies and Mr. King."
     Deborah L. Notkin, "Stephen King: Horror and
       Humanity for Our Time."
     Charles L. Grant, "The Gray Arena."
     Ben P. Indick, "King and the Literary Tradi-
       tion of Horror and the Supernatural."
     Alan Ryan, "The Marston House in 'Salem's
       Lot."
     Douglas E. Winter, "The Night Journeys of
       Stephen King."
     Marty Ketchum, Daniel J. H. Levack, and Jeff
       Levin, "Stephen King: A Bibliography."
     George A. Romero, "Afterword."
Van Hise, James. Enterprise Incidents Presents
Stephen King. Tampa FL: New Media, 1984. Maga-
zine format.
Winter, Douglas E. The Reader's Guide to Stephen
King. Mercer Island WA: Starmont House, 1982.
---------- Stephen King: The Art of Darkness.
New York: NAL, 1984.
Zagorski, Edward J. Teacher's Manual: The Novels
of Stephen King. New York: NAL, 1981 [pamph-
let].

2. Newsletters:

Castle Rock: The Stephen King Newsletter.

Ed. Stephanie Leonard (King´s secretary).
Monthly; newspaper format. First issue,
January 1985. Subscription rates: $15.00
per year (beginning 1986). Address: Castle
Rock, PO Box 8183, Bangor ME 04401.
King´s Crypt.
Eds. William Geoghegan and Tom Simon.
Monthly Newsletter. First issue, July
1985. Subscription rates: $1.00 per issue,
$10.00 for 12 issues. Address: King´s
Crypt, 706 S. Fairifax Street. Alexandria
VA 22314.

3. Selected Critical Articles and Reviews:

Adams, Michael. "Danse Macabre." In Magill´s Lit-
erary Annual 1982, Vol. I. Ed. Frank N. Ma-
gill. Englewood Cliffs NJ: Salem Press, 1982.
Albertson, Jim and Peter S. Perakos. "The
Shining." Cinefantastique, Vol. 7, Nos. 3/4
(1978).
Alexander, Alex E. "Stephen King´s Carrie--A Uni-
versal Fairy Tale." Journal of Popular Culture
(Fall 1969).
Allen, Mel. "The Man Who Writes Nightmares."
Yankee Magazine (March 1979).
Alpert, Michael. "Designing The Eyes of the
Dragon." Castle Rock (August 1985).
Ashley, Mike. "Stephen King." In Who´s Who in Hor-
ror and Fantasy Fiction. New York: Taplinger,
1977.
Atchity, Kenneth. "Stephen King: Making Burgers
With the Best." Los Angeles Times Book Review
20 August 1982.
"Bachman Revealed to be Stephen King Alias." Pub-
lishers Weekly 22 March 1985
Bagnato, Teresa. "´Shining´ at the Overlook
Hotel." Castle Rock (February-March, May 1985).
Bandler, Michael J. "The Horror Is as Much Politi-
cal as Biological." Newsday 19 October 1980.
---------- "The King of the Macabre at Home."
Parents (January 1982).
Barkham, John. "A Story Fired with Imagination,
Protest." Philadelphia Inquirer 31 August 1980.
Barron, Neil. "´Bachman´ Indeed Reads Like Stephen
King." Fantasy Review (March 1985). Review of
Thinner.
---------- "Review of "The Mist" (cassette re-

cording). <u>Fantasy Review</u> (February 1985)

Barry, Dave. "Christine Is Demon for Punishment." <u>Philadelphia Inquirer</u> 27 March 1983.

Beahm, George. "Collecting Stephen King Limiteds." <u>Castle Rock</u> (May 1985).

Bentkowski, Kent Daniel. "A Skeleton Crew Inside King's Closet." <u>Castle Rock</u> (August 1985).

Bishop, Michael. "Mad Dogs . . . and Englishmen." <u>Washington Post Book World</u> 23 August, 1981; as "The Saint Bernard That Becomes an Engine of Madness and Death." <u>San Francisco Chronicle Review</u> 20 September 1981.

Boonstra, John. "King of the Creeps." <u>Hartford Advocate</u> 27 October 1982.

Bradley, Marion Zimmer. "Fandom: Its Value to the Professional." In <u>Inside Outer Space</u>. Ed. Sharon Jarvis. New York: Ungar, 1985. References to King and fandom.

Briggs, Joe Bob. "Big Steve is the Cat's Pajamas." <u>USA Today</u> 8 May 1985. Review of <u>Cat's Eye</u>.

Brown, Stephen. "The Real Beginning of the Real Bachman." <u>Castle Rock</u> (May 1985).

---------- "Stephen King, Shining Through." <u>Washington Post</u> 9 April 1985.

---------- "The Works of Richard Bachman." <u>Washington Post</u> 9 April 1984.

Bryant, Edward. "The Future in Words." <u>Mile High Futures</u> (May 1983; January 1984). Review of <u>Pet Sematary</u>.

Budrys, Algis. "Books." <u>The Magazine of Fantasy and Science Fiction</u> (February 1983).

---------- "A Doggy New Novel from Stephen King." <u>Chicago Sun-Times</u> 6 September 1981.

---------- "King's <u>Firestarter</u>: It's Hot Stuff, All Right." <u>Chicago Sun-Times</u> 21 September 1980.

---------- "Stephen King's Car: Repossessed by the Devil." <u>Chicago Sun-Times Book Week</u> 3 April 1983.

---------- "The Wolf-Mask of Horror, As Lifted by Stephen King." <u>Chicago Sun-Times Book Week</u> 3 May 1981.

Callendar, Newgate. "Criminals at Large." <u>New York Times Book Review</u> 26 May 1974.

Cannon, Leslie. "Where the Conscious Meets the Subconscious." <u>Cincinnati Enquirer</u> 6 April 1978.

Carmichael, Carrie. "Who's Afraid of Stephen

(Carrie) King?" Family Weekly 6 January 1980.
Carter, Erskine. "King is Dead. Long Live the
Kings." Castle Rock (September 1985).
Casey, Susan. "On the Set of ´Salem´s Lot."
Fangoria (February 1980).
"Cat´s Eye Reviews." Castle Rock (June 1985).
Chandler, Randy. "Horror Master Tells Motor-
Vating Tale." Atlanta Journal-Constitution 17
April 1983.
"Checking In: Stephen King." Boston Magazine
(October 1980).
Cheuse, Alan. "Horror Writer´s Holiday." New York
Times Book Review 29 August 1982.
Childs, Mike and Alan Jones. "De Palma Has the
Power." Cinefantastique (Summer 1977).
Chow, Dan. "Locus Looks at More Books." Locus (Ap-
ril 1983).
Christensen, Dan. "Stephen King: Living in
´Constant Deadly Terror.´" Bloody Best of
Fangoria (1982).
Chute, David. "King Gives Second-Best Horror Ef-
fort in ´Cujo.´" Los Angeles Herald Examiner 9
September 1981.
----------- "Reign of Horror." Boston Phoenix 9
December 1980.
Clayton, Bill and Debra Clayton. "Stephen King:
The King of the Beasties." Chillers (November
1981).
Cline, Edward. "Dark Doings in King Country."
Wall Street Journal 28 October 1983.
Collings, Michael R. "Collings Studies Stephen
King." Castle Rock: The Stephen King Newsletter
(June 1985): 8-9. Excerpt from Stephen King as
Richard Bachman.
---------- "Filling the Niche: Genre in Contem-
porary Horror Fantasy." Presented to the Eaton
Conference on Fantasy and Science Fiction,
April 1985.
---------- Letter. Castle Rock (September 1985).
Review article on two films: The Boogeyman and
The Woman in the Room.
--------- "Stephen King´s The Stand: Science Fic-
tion into Fantasy." Presented to the Interna-
tional Conference on the Fantastic in the Arts,
March 1984; In Discovering Stephen King. Ed.
Darrell Schweitzer. Mercer Island WA: Starmont
House, 1985.
--------- Review of Skeleton Crew. Fantasy Review

164

(June 1985).

Collins, Robert A. "Weinberg Gets Last Laugh." Fantasy Review (March 1985).

Collins, Tom. "Frank Belknap Long on Literature, Lovecraft, and the Golden Age of 'Weird Tales.'" Twilight Zone Magazine (January 1982). Assessment of King as modern writer.

Cortland, Will. "The King of Bumps in the Night." Dodge Adventurer (Spring 1985); Castle Rock (June 1985).

Counts, Kyle. Review of Children of the Corn. Cinefantastique (September 1984).

--------- Review of Cujo (film). Cinefantastique (December/January 1983/1984).

Cruz, Manny. "Search for Terror is Worth King's Ransom." Castle Rock (September 1985).

Davis, Joanne. "Trade News: Bachman Revealed to Be Stephen King Alias." Publishers Weekly 22 March 1985.

Davis, L. J. "A Shabby Dog Story from Stephen King." Chicago Tribune Book World 16 August 1981.

De Lint, Charles. Review of The Eyes of the Dragon. Fantasy Review (July 1985).

Demarest, Michael. "Hot Moppet." Time 15 September 1980.

Dimeo, Steve. "Firestarter." Cinefantastique (January 1985).

Disch, Thomas. "Books." Twilight Zone (April 1984).

Doubleday advertisement. Conference program. International Conference on the Fantastic in the Arts. Boca Raton FL. March 1984. Comments on Pet Sematary.

Dudley, Alberta. "My First Science Fiction Convention." Castle Rock (September 1985). King books on sale at convention.

Edwards, Phil. "The Shining." Starburst (1980).

Egan, James. "Apocalypticism in the Fiction of Stephen King." Extrapolation (Fall 1984).

Ehlers, Leigh A. "Carrie: Book and Film." Literature Film Quarterly (Spring 1981.

Ellis, Ray and Katalin Ellis. "The Night of the Horror King." Cinefantastique (May 1985).

Eng, Steve. "Fantasy Writers Focus of Study." The Tennessean Sunday Bookcase 23 January 1983. Review of Fear Itself and Winter's The Reader's Guide to Stephen King.

Everett, David. "Stephen King´s Children of the Corn." _Fangoria_, 35 (April 1984).
---------- "Stephen King´s _Silver Bullet_." _Fangoria_, 48 (1985).
---------- "Of Roaches and Snakes." _Fangoria_, 20 (May 1982). Discussion of Ray Mendez´ work on _Creepshow_.
Fantasy Mongers 13 (Winter 1984/1985): 5. Review of Winter´s _The Art of Darkness_.
---------- 13 (Winter 1984/1985): 5. Review of _Thinner_.
"Fantasy Review Article is a Hoax!" _Castle Rock_ (June 1985).
Ferguson, Mary. "Strawberry Spring: Stephen King´s Gothic Universe." _Footsteps V_ (April 1985).
Fiedler, Leslie. "Fantasy as Commodity, Pornography, Camp and Myth." Presented to the International Conference on the Fantastic in the Arts, March 1984; _Fantasy Review_ (June 1984).
Fleischer, Leonore. "Big Bucks." _Publishers Weekly_ 6 September 1985.
Foltz, Kim and Penelope Wang. "An Unstoppable Thriller King." _Newsweek_ 10 June 1985.
Frane, Jeff. "_Locus_ Looks at More Books." _Locus_ (August 1982).
---------- "A Stunning Storyteller." _Seattle Times Magazine_ 4 February 1979.
Frank, Janrae. "Stephen King´s _Night Shift_: Student Shorts of Stephen King Tales Headed for Videocassette Release." _Cinefantastique_ (July 1985).
French, Lawrence. "_Cat´s Eye_." _Cinefantastique_ (October 1985). Review.
Gagne, Paul. "Catching up with the Rapidly Rising Star of Author Stephen King: Thoughts on Books, Films, and What Went Wrong on _The Shining_." _Cinefantastique_, Vol. 10, No. 4 (1980).
---------- "_Creepshow_: Five Jolting Tales of Horror! from Stephen King and George Romero." _Cinefantastique_ (April 1982).
---------- "_Creepshow_: It´s an $8 Million Comic Book, from George Romero and Friends." _Cinefantastique_ (September/October 1982).
---------- "_Creepshow_: Masters of the Macabre." _Cinefantastique_ (September/October 1982).
---------- "_Salem´s Lot_." _Famous Monsters of Filmland_ (April 1980).

---------- "Stephen King." <u>Cinefantastique</u>, Vol. 10, No. 4 (1980).

---------- "Stephen King." <u>Cinefantastique</u> (December/January 1983-84).

---------- "Stephen King: The Master of the Horror Novel Abandons Television and Turns to Writing for the Screen." <u>Cinefantastique</u>, Vol. 10, No. 1 (1980).

Garcia, Guy D. "People." <u>Time</u> 9 September 1985. Comments on <u>Maximum Overdrive</u>.

Gareffa, Peter M. <u>Stephen King.</u>" Contemporary Authors, New Revision Series, I.

Geoghegan, Bill and Tom Simon. Editorials and columns in <u>King's Crypt</u>. From July 1985.

Gifford, Thomas. "Stephen King's Quartet." <u>Washington Post Book World.</u> 22 August 1982.

Goldberg, Lee. "Now Re-Entering 'The Twilight Zone.'" <u>Starlog</u>, 99 (October 1985). References to King.

Goldstein, Toby. "Stephen King's Scary Monsters Live Right Next Door." <u>Creem</u> (October 1982).

Goodwin, Michael. "The 'Film Script as Novel' Scam." <u>Boulevards</u> (January 1981).

Gorner, Peter. "King Drives at Horror with Less-Than-Usual Fury." <u>Chicago Tribune</u> 6 April 1983.

Goshagarian, Gary. "Goshagarian Finds the Real Stephen King." <u>Castle Rock</u> (August 1985). Address presented to the Hartford College of Women, 24 April 1985.

Graham, Mark. "Critics Dissect Horror of Stephen King's Work." Rocky Mountain News. Review of <u>Fear Itself</u>.

---------- "A Dance into Horror with Stephen King." <u>Rocky Mountain News</u>.

---------- "'Dark Forces' Anthology of Horror." <u>Rocky Mountain News</u> 5 October 1980.

---------- "'Dark Tower' Shows King in Different Light." <u>Rocky Mountain News</u> 1 August 1982.

---------- "Good News for Horror Buffs." <u>Rocky Mountain News</u> 11 May 1984. Review of <u>Shadowings</u>.

---------- "Macabre Master." <u>Rocky Mountain News</u> 4 December 1983. Review of <u>Pet Sematary</u> and <u>Cycle of the Werewolf</u>.

---------- "Masters of the Macabre." <u>Rocky Mountain News</u> 7 October 1984. Review of <u>The Talisman</u>.

---------- "Moral Dilemma in Latest Novel by Stephen King." <u>Rocky Mountain News</u> 9 September 1979. Review of <u>The Dead Zone</u>.

---------- "Mouth Foaming for Good Scare?" <u>Rocky Mountain News</u> 6 September 1981.

---------- "New King Novel Will Frighten You." <u>Rocky Mountain News</u> 14 September 1980. Review of <u>Firestarter</u>.

---------- "Revealing Work Examines King-Bachman Connection." <u>Rocky Mountain News</u> 15 September 1985. Review of <u>Stephen King as Richard Bachman</u>.

---------- "Stephen King Causes a ´Fury´ of a Monster, 1958 Vintage." <u>Rocky Mountain News</u> 8 May 1983.

---------- "Stephen King Shows Another Grisly Side." <u>Rocky Mountain News</u> 19 September 1982. Review of <u>Different Seasons.</u>

---------- "Stephen King Stories Never Seem to Die." <u>Rocky Mountain News</u> 16 June 1985. Review of <u>Skeleton Crew</u>.

Granger, Bill. "Stephen King Strikes Again." <u>Chicago Tribune Book World</u> 24 August 1980.

Grant, Charles L., David Morrell, Alan Ryan, and Douglas E. Winter. "Different Writers on <u>Different Seasons</u>. <u>Fantasy Newsletter</u> (February 1983); in <u>Shadowings</u>. Ed. Douglas E. Winter. Mercer Island WA: Starmont House, 1983

Grant, Donald M. "Stephen King as Breckinridge Elkins?" <u>Castle Rock</u> (May 1985).

---------- "Some Reflections on Specialty Publishing." <u>Castle Rock</u> (May 1985).

Gray, Paul. "Master of Postliterate Prose." <u>Time</u> 20 August 1982.

Grobaty, Tim. "Stephen King Thinks It´s Fun to ´Get the Reader.´" <u>Watertown Daily Times</u> 18 September 1980.

Hall, Melissa Mia. "A Bestseller that Foams at the Mouth." <u>Fort Worth Star-Telegram</u> 23 August 1981.

Hansen, Ron. "<u>Creepshow</u>: The Dawn of a Living Horror Comedy." <u>Esquire</u> (January 1981).

Hard, Annette. "King: Novellas from a Consummate Story Teller." <u>Houston Chronicle</u> 12 September 1982.

Harper, L. Christine. "Christine" (Reel Futures). <u>Mile High Futures</u> 22 January 1984.

Harris, Judith. P. "Timid, One-Note Stories need Padding to Fill Even 30 Minutes." <u>Cinefantas-</u>

tique (July 1985). Review of <u>Tales from the
Darkside</u> ("The Word Processor").
---------- "King: Sailing Uncharted Seas." <u>Hous-
ton Chronicle</u> 7 October 1979.
Hatlen, Burton. "Alumnus Publishes Symbolic
Novel, Shows Promise." <u>The Maine Campus</u> 12 Ap-
ril 1974.
Hatlen, Burton. "The Destruction and Re-Creation
of the Human Community in Stephen King's <u>The
Stand</u>." Presented to the International Confer-
ence on the Fantastic in the Arts, March 1984;
<u>Footsteps V</u> (April 1982).
---------- "The Mad Dog and Maine." In <u>Shadow-
ings</u>. Ed. Douglas E. Winter. Mercer Island WA:
Starmont House, 1983.
---------- "´Salem's Lot Critiques American Civ-
ilization." <u>The Maine Campus</u> 12 December 1975.
---------- "Steve King's <u>The Stand</u>." <u>Kennebec</u>
(April 1979).
---------- "Steve King's Third Novel Shines On."
<u>The Maine Campus</u> 1 April 1977.
Heldreth, Leonard. "King's ´The Body´: A Portrait
of the Artist as Survivor." Manuscript article.
Herndon, Ben. "Real Tube Terror." <u>Twilight Zone
Magazine</u> (December 1985).
Hewitt, Tim. "Cat's Eye." <u>Cinefantastique</u> (May
1985).
---------- "Cat's Eye." <u>Cinefantastique</u> (October
1985).
---------- "Silver Bullet." <u>Cinefantastique</u> (May
1985).
Hofsess, John. "Kubrick: Critics Be Damned." <u>Soho
News</u> (NY) 28 May 1980.
Hogan, David J. "<u>The Dead Zone</u>." <u>Cinefantastique</u>
(December/January 1983/1984).
---------- "<u>Firestarter</u>." <u>Cinefantastique</u> (Sep-
tember 1984).
---------- "King and Cronenberg: It's the Best of
Both Worlds." <u>Cinefantastique</u> (December
1983/January 1984).
Horsting, Jessica. "<u>Cat's Eye</u>. <u>Fantastic Films</u>
(June 1985).
---------- "<u>Cujo</u>: The Movie." <u>Fantastic Films</u> (No-
vember 1983).
Indick, Ben P. "Stephen King As an Epic Writer."
In <u>Discovering Modern Horror Fiction, I.</u> Ed.
Darrell Schweitzer. Mercer Island WA: Starmont
House, 1985.

Johnson, Kim. "Christine: Stephen King and John
    Carpenter Take a Joy Ride into Terror!" Media-
    scene Prevue (1983).
Kaveney, Roz. "The Consolations of Terror." Books
    & Bookmen (November 1981).
Keeler, Greg. "The Shining: Ted Kramer Has a
    Nightmare." Journal of Popular Film and Tele-
    vision (Winter 1981).
Kelley, Bill. "Cat´s Eye." Cinefantastique (July
    1985).
---------- "John Carpenter´s Christine: Bringing
    Stephen King´s Best Seller to the Screen."
    Cinefantastique (September 1983).
---------- "King´s ´Firestarter´ Stretches Boun-
    daries of Macabre Fiction." Fort Lauderdale
    News/Sun Sentinel 28 September 1980.
---------- "´Salem´s Lot: Filming Horror for
    Television." Cinefantastique (Winter 1979).
Kendrick, Walter. "Stephen King Gets Eminent."
    Village Voice 29 April/ 5 May 1981.
Kennedy, Harlan. "Kubrick Goes Gothic." American
    Film (June 1980).
Kilbourne, Dan. "Christine." In Magill´s Cinema
    Annual 1984. Ed. Frank N. Magill. Englewood
    Cliffs NY: Salem Press, 1984.
King, Tabitha. "Living with the Bogey Man." In
    Murderess, Ink. Ed. Dilys Winn. New York:
    Bell, 1979.
"King New Book Advance--$1.00." Locus (January
    1983).
"King´s Too Fast for His Own Good." Los Angeles
    Daily News 11 April 1985.
Klein, Jeanne. "King Recycles a Chilling Tale."
    Seattle Post-Intelligencer 6 May 1985.
Kroll, Jack. "Stanley Kubrick´s Horror Show."
    Newsweek 26 May 1980.
Lawson, Carol. "Stephen King." The New York
    Times Book Review 23 September 1979.
Leerhsen, Charles. "The Titans of Terror." News-
    week 24 December 1984: 61-62. King and Straub.
Lehmann-Haupt, Christopher. "Books of the Times."
    New York Times 17 August 1979; as "What If You
    Could Know the Future?" Seattle Post-Intelli-
    gencer 26 August 1979.
---------- "Books of the Times." New York Times 8
    September 1980; as "This Girl May Set World
    Afire." Omaha World-Herald 14 September 1980;
    as "A Little Girl´s Pyrotechnics." Seattle

Post-Intelligencer 21 September 1980.
---------- "Books of the Times." New York Times
14 April 1981; as "´Danse Macabre to Appeal to
Lovers of Grisly Stories." Omaha World-Herald
26 April 1981.
---------- "Books of the Times." New York Times
14 August 1981.
---------- "Books of the Times." New York Times
11 August 1982.
---------- "Books of the Times." New York Times
12 April 1983.
---------- "Books of the Times." New York Times
21 October 1983; as "Finally, a Story to Scare
Stephen King." Denver Post 30 October 1983.
Leiber, Fritz. "Fantasy Books." Locus (April
1980). Review of The Dead Zone.
---------- "On Fantasy." Fantasy Newsletter, No.
39 (August 1981).
---------- "Whispering in the Shadows." Washing-
ton Post Book World 12 April 1981.
Leonard, Stephanie. Editorials and columns in
Castle Rock: The Stephen King Newsletter. From
January 1985.
---------- "Stephen King Bibliography," Parts I
and II. Castle Rock (June/ July 1985).
Levin, Martin. "Genre Items." New York Times Book
Review 4 February 1979.
Lingeman, Richard R. "Something Nasty in the Tub."
New York Times 1 March 1977.
Lorenz, Janet. "Carrie." In Magill´s Survey of
Cinema. 2nd series. Vol. I. Ed. Frank N. Ma-
gill. Englewood Cliffs NJ: Salem Press, 1981.
Lucas, Tim. "David Cronenberg´s The Dead Zone."
Cinefantastique 14, No 2 (December/January
1983/1984).
---------- and editors of Video Times. Your Movie
Guide to Horror Video Tapes and Discs. Publi-
cations International, 1985.
Luciano, Dale. "Danse Macabre: Stephen King Sur-
veys the Field of Horror." The Comics Journal,
No. 72 (May 1982).
---------- "E.C. Horror Stories Mistranslated into
Film." The Comics Journal, No. 79 (January
1983).
Lyons, Gene. "King of High-School Horror." News-
week 2 May 1983.
McDonnell, David. "The Once and Future King." Pre-
vue (May 1982).

McDonnell, David and John Sayers. "Creepshow."
    Mediascene Prevue (May 1982).
McDowell, Edwin. "Behind the Bestsellers." New
    York Times Book Review 27 September 1981.
McLellan, Joseph. "Vision of Holocaust." Washing-
    ton Post 30 August 1979.
Macklin, F. Anthony. "Understanding Kubrick: The
    Shining." Journal of Popular Television and
    Film (Summer 1981).
Magistrale, Anthony S. "Inherited Haunts: Stephen
    King's Terrible Children." Extrapolation
    (Spring 1985).
---------- "Stephen King's Vietnam Allegory: an
    Interpretation of 'Children of the Corn.'" Pre-
    sented to the International Conference on the
    Fantastic in the Arts, March 1984; Cuyahoga Re-
    view (Spring/Summer 1984): 61-66; Footsteps V
    (April 1985).
Malpezzi, Frances M. and William M. Clements. "The
    Shining." In Magill's Survey of Cinema. 2nd
    Series. Vol. V. Ed. Frank N. Magill. Engle-
    wood Cliffs NJ: Salem Press, 1981.
Martin, Robert. "A Casual Chat with Mr. George A.
    Romero." Fangoria (October 1982).
---------- "Creepshow." Twilight Zone Magazine
    (September 1982).
---------- "Interview with a Werewolf." Fangoria,
    No. 44 (1985).
---------- "Keith Gordon and Christine." Fangoria,
    No. 32 (1983).
---------- "Mark Lester Directs Firestarter." Fan-
    goria 36 (1984).
---------- "On (and Off) the Set of Creepshow."
    Fangoria (July 1982).
---------- "On the Set of Firestarter." Fangoria
    35 (1984).
---------- "Richard Kobritz and Christine." Fan-
    goria, No. 32 (1983).
---------- "Stephen King's Silver Bullet." Fangor-
    ia, No. 48 (1985).
Mayer, Sheryl. "An Evening with Stephen King at
    Amherst." Castle Rock (May 1985).
Mewshaw, Michael. "Novels and Stories." New York
    Times Book Review 26 March 1978.
"A Mild Down-Easter Discovers Terror Is the
    Ticket." People 29 December 1980-5 January
    1981.
Moore, Darrell. The Best, Worst, and Most Unusual

<u>Horror Films</u>. Skokie IL: Publications Interna-
tional, 1983 (hardcover). <u>Carrie</u>: 93, 128; <u>The
Shining</u>.
Moritz, Charles. "Stephen King." <u>Contemporary
Biography Yearbook 1981</u>. New York: H. H. Wil-
son, 1981.
Morrison, Michael A. "Pet Sematary: Opposing Views
. . . Finest Horror Ever Written." <u>Fantasy Re-
view</u>, No. 64 (January 1984).
Munster, Bill. "An Interview with Douglas E.
Winter." <u>Footsteps V</u> (April 1985).
Naha, Ed. "Front Row Seats at the <u>Creepshow</u>." <u>Twi-
light Zone Magazine</u> (May 1982).
Nathan, Paul. S. "Helping Hand." <u>Publishers Weekly</u>
30 August 1985.
---------- "<u>The Talisman</u> and the Clubs." <u>Publish-
ers Weekly</u> 23 November 1984.
Neilson, Keith. "<u>The Dead Zone</u>." In <u>Magill's Lit-
erary Annual 1980</u>, Vol. I. Ed. Frank N.
Magill. Englewood Cliffs NJ: Salem Press, 1980
(hardcover).
---------- "<u>Different Seasons</u>." In <u>Magill's
Literary Annual 1983</u>, Vol. I. Ed. Frank N.
Magill. Englewood Cliffs NJ: Salem Press,
1983 (hardcover).
---------- "King Gets Compatible Critic." <u>Fantasy
Review</u> (March 1985): 15-16. Review of Winter's
<u>Stephen King: The Art of Darkness</u>.
Neuhaus, Cable. "<u>Firestarter</u>'s Premier Was a Crit-
ical Fizzle. . . ." <u>People</u> 28 May 1984.
Norulak, Frank. "Searching for Richard Bachman."
<u>Castle Rock</u> (September 1985).
Novak, Ralph. "Firestarter." <u>People</u> 28 May 1984.
Osbourne, Linda B. "The Supernatural Con Man vs.
the Hymn-Singing Mother." <u>Washington Post</u> 23
November 1978.
Patrouch, Jr., Joseph F. "Stephen King in Con-
text." In <u>Patterns of the Fantastic</u>. Ed. Don-
ald M. Hassler. Mercer Island WA: Starmont
House, 1983.
Pautz, Peter J. Review of <u>Christine</u>. <u>Science
Fiction & Fantasy Book Review</u> (SFRA), No. 16
(July-August 1983).
Pettus, David, ed. <u>Fan Plus</u>. 1984. Stephen King
issue.
Phippen, Sanford. "Stephen King's Appeal to
Youth." <u>Maine Life</u> (December 1980).
Podhoretz, John. "The Magnificent Revels of

Stephen King." <u>Wall Street Journal</u> 4 September 1980.

Price, Robert M. "T.E.D. Klein." In <u>Discovering Modern Horror Fiction, I</u>. Ed. Darrell Schweitzer. Mercer Island WA: Starmont House, 1985. Discussion of "The Mist" (80).

Proch, Paul and Charles Kaufman. "Eggboiler." <u>National Lampoon</u> (May 1984): 32-37, 48, 54, 70. Parody of <u>Firestarter</u>.

Radburn, Barry. "Stephen King and John Carpenter: Cruisin´ with Christine." <u>Footsteps V</u> (April 1985).

Rebeaux, Max. "Twilight Zone." <u>Cinefantastique</u> 15 (October 1985).

Reuter, Madalynne. "502,000 Copies of <u>Talisman</u> Shipped in One Day." <u>Publishers Weekly</u> 26 October 1984.

Riggenbach, Jeff. "Suspense Accelerates in King´s <u>Christine</u>." <u>San Jose Mercury News</u> 1 May 1983.

Rolfe, John. "Fitting Author Stephen King to the Charles Dickens Mold." <u>Maine Sunday Telegram</u> 19 September 1982.

Roraback, Dick. "Gift of Sight: Visions from a Nether World." <u>Los Angeles Times Book Review</u> 26 August 1979.

Rosenbaum, Mary Helene. "Pet Sematary." <u>Christian Century</u> 21 March 1984.

Ryan, Alan. "Ride into Horror with ´Christine.´" <u>Cleveland Plain Dealer</u> 17 April 1983.

Ryan, Desmond. "The Scariest Movie Ever Made." <u>Saga</u> (July 1980).

---------- "Stephen King Departs from Horror." <u>Cleveland Plain Dealer</u> 26 September 1982.

Salamon, Julie. "Horrormonger Stephen King on Screen." <u>Wall Street Journal</u> 25 April 1985. Review of <u>Cat´s Eye</u>.

Sallee, Wayne Allen. "No Bones About It." <u>Castle Rock</u> (August 1985). Review of <u>Skeleton Crew</u>.

---------- "<u>Thinner</u>: A Thinly Disguised King Novel." <u>Castle Rock</u> (May 1985).

Sanders, Joe. Review of <u>The Talisman</u>. <u>Fantasy Review</u> (February 1985).

Scapperotti, Dan. "Tales from the Darkside." <u>Cinefantastique</u> (January 1985).

Schiff, Stuart David. "The Glorious Past, Erratic Present, and Questionable Future of the Specialty Presses." In <u>Inside Outer Space</u>. Ed. Sharon Jarvis. New York: Ungar, 1985.

Schneider, Peter. "Collecting the Works of Stephen King." <u>AB Bookman's Weekly</u> 24 October 1983.

Schow, David J. "Return of the Curse of the Son of Mr. King: Book Two." <u>Whispers</u>, No. 17/18 (August 1982).

Schweitzer, Darrell. "Introduction." In <u>Discovering Modern Horror Fiction, I</u>. Ed. Darrell Schweitzer. Mercer Island WA: Starmont House, 1985. King's influence on horror fiction.

Science Fiction Book Club brochure. "Stephen King." August 1985.

Scott, Pete. "The Shadow Exploded." <u>Dark Horizons</u> (Summer 1982).

See, Carolyn. "A Bumper Crop of Killing." <u>Los Angeles Times</u> 8 May 1983.

Seelye, John. "Wizard of Ooze with Four Novellas Makes Poe a Piker." <u>Chicago Tribune Bookworld</u> 22 August 1982.

Sherman, David. "Nightmare Library." <u>Fangoria</u> (April 1984). Review of <u>Cycle</u>.

---------- "Nightmare Library." <u>Fangoria</u>, No. 44 (1985): 39-40. Review of <u>The Talisman</u>.

Shiner, Lewis. "A Collision of Good and Evil." <u>Dallas Morning News</u> 26 November 1978.

Shreffler, Philip A. "For Chills and Thrills." <u>St. Louis Post-Dispatch</u> 5 October 1980.

Slung, Michelle. "A Master of the Macabre." <u>The New Republic</u> 21 February 1981; expanded as "In the Matter of Stephen King." <u>Armchair Detective</u> (Spring 1981); rpt. <u>Castle Rock</u> (September 1985).

---------- "Scare Tactics." <u>New York Times Book Review</u> 10 May 1981.

Smith, Joan. "Pseudonym Kept Five King Novels a Mystery." <u>Bangor Daily News</u> 9 February 1985.

Smith, Roger. "The Uncrowning of King." <u>State of Shock</u> (April 1981).

Squires, Roy A. "Science Fiction and Fantasy: An Overview." <u>AB Bookman's Weekly</u> 24 October 1983. Reference to King.

Sragow, Michael. "Stephen King's 'Creepshow': The Aesthetics of Gross-out." <u>Rolling Stone</u> 25 November 1982.

Stamm, Michael E. Review of <u>Cycle of the Werewolf</u>. <u>Science Fiction & Fantasy Review</u> (March 1984).

---------- "Pet Sematary: Opposing Views . . . Flawed, Unsatisfying." <u>Fantasy Review</u>, No. 64

(January 1984).

---------- Review of <u>Pet Sematary</u>. <u>Science Fiction & Fantasy Book Review</u> (SFRA), No. 20 (December 1983).

Stasio, Marilyn. "High Suspense." <u>Penthouse</u> (July 1983).

"Stephen King." <u>Contemporary Literary Criticism</u>, Vol. 12. Eds. Dedria Bryfonski and Garard Senick. Detroit MI: Gale Research, 1980.

"Stephen King." <u>Current Biography Yearbook, 1981</u>. Ed. Charles Moritz. New York: H. W. Wilson, 1981.

"Stephen King Makes Millions by Scaring Hell Out of Three Million Readers." <u>People</u> 7 March 1981.

"Stephen King's Torrent of Horror." <u>USA Today</u> 11 July 1985.

"Straub Talks About <u>Talisman</u>. <u>Castle Rock</u> (July 1985).

Strouse, Jean. "Beware of the Dog." <u>Newsweek</u> 31 August 1981.

Sullivan, Jack. "Two Ways to Write a Gothic." <u>New York Times Book Review</u> 20 February 1977.

Suplee, Curt. "Stricken a la King." <u>Washington Post</u> 26 August 1980.

Thompson, Andrea. "The Thrills, Chills, and Skills of Stephen King." <u>McCall's</u> (February 1983).

Thompson, Thomas. "King's Latest a Shaggy Rabid Dog Story." <u>Los Angeles Times</u> 6 September 1981; as "'Cujo': Tale About a Mad Dog Ought to be Put to Sleep." <u>Baltimore News American</u> 6 September 1981.

Tuchman, Michael. "From Niagara-on-the-Lake, Ontario." <u>Film Comment</u>, 19, No. 3 (May-June 1983). Interview with Cronenberg on <u>The Dead Zone</u>.

Van Rjndt, Phillipe. "The Other Woman Was a Car." <u>New York Times Book Review</u> 3 April 1983.

Vernier, James. "<u>Christine</u>." <u>Twilight Zone Magazine</u> (February 1984).

---------- "On the Set of <u>Dead Zone</u>." <u>Twilight Zone Magazine</u> (December 1983).

---------- "Zeroing in on <u>The Dead Zone</u>." <u>Twilight Zone Magazine</u> (November/December 1983).

Wells, Jeffrey. "'Creepshow' Crawlers Can Cause Creepy Cold Chills." <u>New York Post</u> 3 September 1981.

Wiater, Stanley. "Danse Macabre." <u>Valley Advocate</u>

27 May 1981.

---------- "Dark Stars Rising." Valley Advocate 8
April 1981.

---------- "Just Your Average Guy." Valley Advocate 27 May 1981.

---------- "Stephen King and George Romero: Collaboration in Terror." Fangoria (June 1980).

---------- "Stephen King and George Romero." Fangoria (1982).

Williams, Paul. "Fit for a King: Fascination with
Horror Stories." Los Angeles Times 10 May 1981.

Williams, Sharon. "Stephen King´s Cycle of the
Werewolf Becomes Silver Bullet for the Silver
Screen." Fantastic Films (October 1985).

Willis, John. "Christine." In Screen World 1984.
New York: Crown, 1984. Pictorial review.

---------- "Creepshow." In Screen World 1983. New
York: Crown, 1983.

---------- "Cujo." In Screen World 1984. New York:
Crown, 1984.

---------- "The Dead Zone." In Screen World 1984.
New York: Crown, 1984. Pictorial review.

---------- "The Shining." In Screen World 1981.
New york: Crown, 1981. Pictorial review.

Wilson, F. Paul. "TZ Terror." Twilight Zone Magazine (December 1985).

Winter, Douglas E. "The Art of Darkness." In
Shadowings. Ed. Douglas E. Winter. Mercer Island WA: Starmont House.

---------- Excerpt from The Faces of Fear. In
Castle Rock (May 1985).

---------- "I Want My Cake! Thoughts on Creepshow
and E.C. Comics." In Shadowings Ed. Douglas E.
Winter. Mercer Island WA: Starmont House, 1983.

---------- "Pet Sematary." Washington Post Book
World 13 November 1983.

---------- "Shadowings: Firestarter by Stephen
King." Fantasy Newsletter, No. 30 (November
1980).

---------- "Stephen King, Peter Straub, and the
Quest for The Talisman." Twilight Zone Magazine
(January/February 1985).

---------- "Stephen King´s Christine: . . . where
innocence peels away like burnt rubber and
death rides shotgun." Fantasy Newsletter, No.
56 (February 1983).

---------- "Stephen King´s Cujo: ´Nope, nothing
wrong here.´" Fantasy Newsletter, No. 42 (No-

vember 1981).

---------- "Thoughts on Creepshow and E.C.
Comics." Fantasy Newsletter, No. 56 (February
1983); revised in Shadowings. Ed. Douglas E.
Winter. Mercer Island WA: Starmont House, 1983.

---------- "Winter Reviews Skeleton Crew." Castle
Rock (September 1985). Originally appeared in
the Philadelphia Inquirer 30 June 1985.

Wood, Robin. "King Meets Cronenberg." Canadian
Forum (January 1984).

Woods, Larry D. Review of The Dark Tower: The
Gunslinger. Science Fiction & Fantasy Book Review (SFRA), No. 11 (January-February 1983).

---------- "Stephen King Horrifies Again." Nash-
ville Tennessean 25 December 1984.

Wynorski, Jim. "A New Definition for Ultimate Horror: The Shining." Fangoria (August 1980).

Yardley, Jonathan. "Mean Machine." Washington Post
23 March 1983.

VII. SELECTED INTERVIEWS AND PROFILES

1. Attributed Interviews:

Bellows, Keith, "The King of Terror." Sourcebook:
The Magazine for Seniors (1982).
Cadigan, Pat, Arnie Fenner and Marty Ketchum. "Has
Success Spoiled Stephen King?" Shayol, No. 6
(Winter 1982).
Cavett, Dick, moderator. "Horror Panel", I-II.
New York: WNET. 30-31 October 1980. Tran-
scripts from Journal Graphics, Inc. Discussion
with George Romero, Stephen King, Peter Straub,
and Ira Levin.
Chan, Mei-Mei. "King's Gruesome Ideas are Dead
Serious." USA Today 14 October 1982.
Chute, David. "King of the Night." Take One
(January 1979).
Denver, Joel. "Stephen King Takes a Stand for
Radio." Radio & Records 24 February 1984.
Dewes, Joyce Lynch. "An Interview with Stephen
King." Mystery (March 1981).
Donaldson, Stephen R. "Stephen King." Archon 6
Program Book (July 1982).
Duncan, David D., and others. "The Kings of
Horror." Oui (August 1981).
Fleischer, Leonore. "A Talk With Stephen King."
Washington Post Book World 1 October 1978.
Freff. "The Dark Beyond the Door: Walking
(Nervously) Into Stephen King's World." Tomb of
Dracula 1, No. 4 (April 1980); Part II, Tomb of
Dracula 1, No.5 (June 1980).
Goldstein, William. "A Coupl'a Authors Sittin'
Around Talkin'." Publishers Weekly 11 May 1984.
Grant, Charles. "King-Size Interview," Parts I,
II, III. Monsterland, No. 2-4 (1985).
---------- "Stephen King: I Like to Go for the
Jugular." Twilight Zone Magazine (April 1981).
Herndon, Ben. "New Adventures in the Screen
Trade." Twilight Zone Magazine (December 1985).
Janeczko, Paul. "An Interview with Stephen King."
English Journal (February 1980).
Jones, Stephen. "The Night Shifter: An Interview
with Stephen King." Fantasy Media (March 1979).
Kilday, Gregg. "Reflections on Hollywood with Au-
thor Stephen King." Los Angeles Herald Exam-
iner 23 September 1979.
Lofficier, Randy. "Stephen King Talks About Chris-

tine." <u>Twilight Zone Magazine</u> (January/February 1984).

Lowry, Lois. "King of the Occult." <u>Down East Magazine</u> (November 1977).

Martin, R. H. "Stephen King on <u>Overdrive</u> and <u>Pet Sematary</u> and on Capturing the Spirit." <u>Fangoria</u>, #48 (1985).

Modderno, Craig. "I´d Really Like to Write a Rock ´n´ Roll Novel." <u>USA Today</u> 10 May 1985.

Norden, Eric. "The Playboy Interview: Stephen King." <u>Playboy</u> (June 1983).

Peck, Abe. "Stephen King´s Court of Honor." <u>Rolling Stone College Papers.</u> (Winter 1983).

Perakos, Peter S. "Stephen King on <u>Carrie</u>, <u>The Shining</u>, Etc." <u>Cinefantastique</u>, Vol. 8, No. 1 (1978).

Platt, Charles. "Stephen King." <u>Dream Makers II</u>. New York: Berkley, 1983 (paperback).

Robertson, William. "Writer Stephen King: Horror in a Secular Age." <u>Miami Herald</u> 25 March 1984.

Sherman, David. "The Stephen King Interview." <u>Fangoria</u> 35 (April 1984); 36 (May 1984).

Shiner, Lewis, Marty Ketchum, Arnold Fenner, and Pat Cadigan. "Shine of the Times: An Interview with Stephen King." <u>Shayol</u>, No. 3 (Summer 1979).

Small, Michael. "Peter Straub and Stephen King Team Up for Fear." <u>People</u> 28 January 1985.

Spitz, Bob. "Penthouse Interview: Stephen King." <u>Penthouse</u> (April 1982).

Stein, Michael. "Stephen King." <u>Fantastic Films</u> (February 1983).

Stewart, Robert. "Flix." <u>Heavy Metal</u> (January, February, March 1980).

---------- "The Rest of King." <u>Starship</u> (Spring 1981). Continuation of <u>Heavy Metal</u> interview.

Thomases, Martha, and Robert Tebbel. "Interview: Stephen King." <u>Hightimes</u> (June 1981).

Weaver, Dan. "Interview . . . Stephen King." <u>The Literary Guild Monthly Selection Magazine</u> (December 1978).

Wiater, Stanley and Roger Anker. "Horror Partners." <u>Fangoria</u> 42 (March 1985).

Wilson, William. "Riding the Crest of the Horror Craze." <u>New York Times Magazine</u> 11 May 1980.

Winter, Douglas E. "Horror and the Limits of Violence." In <u>Shadowings</u>. Ed. Douglas E. Winter. Mercer Island WA: Starmont House,

1983.
---------- "Some Words with Stephen King." Fantasy
  Newsletter, No. 56 (February 1983).
---------- "Stephen King's Art of Darkness."
  Fantasy Review (November 1984).

2. Unattributed Interviews:

Bangor Daily News (May 1983). King's first
  interview; discussion of Carrie.
"Front Row Seats at the Creepshow." Twilight Zone
  Magazine (May 1982).
"Horror Teller." Horizon (February 1978).
"Interview: Stephen King." Infinity Cubed, No. 5
  (1980).
"King's Eye." Cinefantastique (May 1985).
"Stephen King." Publishers Weekly 17 January 1977.
"Stephen King Talks about Christine." Twilight
  Zone Magazine (February 1984).
"Witches and Aspirin." Writer's Digest (June
  1977).

For more extensive listings of King's interviews,
see Winter (Art, 230-234); Ketchum, Levack, and
Levin (FI 263-265); and Leonard (CR [June, July
1985]).

LIST OF WORKS CITED

The following list excludes references to King's novels, stories, and published articles, all of which appear in the preceding checklist. Pagination for King's novels is based on first hardcover trade editions, except for two works: <u>Eyes</u>, available only in the limited edition; and <u>Cycle</u>, references to which are keyed to months.

Aldiss, Brian W. <u>Billion Year Spree: The True History of Science Fiction</u>. Garden City NY: Doubleday, 1973.

Anthony, Piers. <u>Blue Adept</u>. New York: Ballantine, 1981.

---------- <u>Split Infinity</u>. New York: Ballantine, 1980.

---------- <u>Juxtaposition</u>. New York: Ballantine, 1982.

Bloch, Robert. "The Strange Flight of Richard Clayton." In <u>Amazing Stories: 60 Years of the Best Science Fiction</u>. Eds. Isaac Asimov and Martin H. Greenberg. Lake Geneva WI: TSR, Inc., 1985. 67-73. Rpt. from <u>Amazing</u>, March 1939.

Brown, Stephen. "Stephen King: Shining Through." <u>Washington Post</u> 9 April 1985.

---------- "The Works of Richard Bachman." <u>Washington Post</u> 9 April 1985: C4.

Bryant, Edward. "The Future in Words." <u>Mile High Futures</u> (January 1984): 18-19.

Collings, Michael R. <u>Stephen King as Richard Bachman</u>. Mercer Island WA: Starmont House, 1985.

---------- "Filling the Niche: Fantasy and Science Fiction in Contemporary Horror." Lloyd J. Eaton Conference, University of California, Riverside. 14 April 1985.

---------- "<u>The Stand</u>: Fantasy into Science Fiction." In <u>Discovering Stephen King</u>. Ed. Darrell Schweitzer. Mercer Island: Starmont House, 1985. 83-90.

Collings, Michael R. and David A. Engebretson. <u>The Shorter Works of Stephen King</u>. Mercer Island WA: Starmont House, 1985.

Collins, Tom. "Frank Belknap Long on Literature, Lovecraft, and the Golden Age of 'Weird

Tales.'" _Twilight Zone Magazine_ (January
    1982): 13-19, esp. 18.
Crawford, Gary William. "Stephen King's American
    Gothic." In _Discovering Stephen King_. Ed.
    Darrell Schweitzer. Mercer Island WA: Star-
    mont House, 1985. 41-45.
De Felitta, Frank. _Golgotha Falls_. New York: Simon
    & Schuster, 1984.
De Lint, Charles. "Privately Published Fantasy
    King's Best." _Fantasy Review_ (July 1985): 19.
    Review of _The Eyes of the Dragon_.
Demarest, Michael. "Hot Moppet." _Time_ 25 September
    1980. Review of _Firestarter_.
Doubleday advertisement. Conference Program. In-
    ternational Conference on the Fantastic in
    the Arts, Boca Raton FL. March 1984.
Fiedler, Leslie. "Fantasy as Commodity, Pornogra-
    phy, Camp, and Myth." _Fantasy Review_ 68
    (June 1984): 6-9, 42.
Foltz, Kim and Penelope Wang. "An Unstoppable
    Thriller King." _Newsweek_ 10 June 1985: 62-
    63.
Gareffa, Peter. "Stephen King." _Contemporary Au-
    thors_, New Revision Series, I. 333-336.
Godwin, Parke. "There Goes Deuteronomy." In _Inside
    Outer Space_. Ed. Sharon Jarvis. New York:
    Ungar, 1985: 3-13.
Goshgarian, Gary. "Goshgarian Finds the Real Ste-
    phen King." _Castle Rock: The Stephen King
    Newsletter_ (August 1985): 1, 5, 7-8.
Grant, Charles L. "Stephen King: I Like to Go for
    the Jugular." _Twilight Zone Magazine_ (April
    1981): 18-23.
Gray, Paul. "Master of Postliterate Prose." _Time_
    20 August 1982: 87.
Griffin, Andrew. "Sympathy for the Werewolf." In
    The Borzoi College Reader. Eds. Charles Mus-
    catine and Marlene Griffith. 5th ed. New
    York: Knopf, 1984. 646-651. Rpt. _University
    Publishing_ (Winter 1979).
Heldreth, Leonard. "The Ultimate Horror: The Dead
    Child in Stephen King's Stories and Novels."
    In _Discovering Stephen King_. Ed. Darrell
    Schweitzer. Mercer Island WA: Starmont
    House, 1985. 141-152.
Indick, Ben P. "King and the Literary Tradition
    of Horror and the Supernatural." In _Fear It-
    self_. Eds. Tim Underwood and Chuck Miller.

New York: NAL/Plume, 1984. 171-186.
---------- "Stephen King as Epic Writer." In <u>Dis-</u>
<u>covering Modern Horror Fiction</u>. Ed. Darrell
Schweitzer. Mercer Island WA: Starmont
House, 1985. 56-67.
---------- "What Makes Him So <u>Scary</u>?" In <u>Discov-</u>
<u>ering Stephen King</u>. Ed. Darrell Schweitzer.
Mercer Island WA: Starmont House, 1985. 9-14.
Jackson, Shirley. <u>The Haunting of Hill House</u>. New
York: Penguin, 1984; rpt. Viking 1959.
Jacobs, W. W. "The Monkey's Paw." In <u>Great Tales</u>
<u>of Terror and the Supernatural</u>. Eds. Herbert
A. Wise and Phyllis Fraser. New York: Modern
Library, 1944. 592-603.
King, Stephen. Letter to Michael R. Collings, 3
August 1985.
"King New Book Advance--$1.00." <u>Locus</u> (January
1985).
Klein, Jeanne. "King Recycles a Chilling Tale."
<u>Seattle Post-Intelligencer</u>. 6 May 1985: B12.
Klein, T. E. D. <u>The Ceremonies</u>. New York: Viking,
1984 [hardcover]; New York: Bantam, 1984 [pa-
perback]. Citations from the Bantam edition.
Lawson, Carol. "Behind the Best Sellers: Stephen
King." <u>New York Times Book Review</u> 23 Septem-
ber 1979: 42.
Leiber, Fritz. "Horror Hits a High." In <u>Fear It-</u>
<u>self: The Horror Fiction of Stephen King</u>.
Eds. Tim Underwood and Chuck Miller. New
York: NAL/Plume, 1984. 103-122.
Lewis, C. S. "On Science Fiction." In <u>Of Other</u>
<u>Worlds</u>. Ed. Walter E. Hooper. New York: Har-
court, Brace, Jovanovich, 1966. 59-73.
Modderno, Craig. "I'd Really Like to Write a Rock
'n' Roll Novel." <u>USA Today</u> 10 May 1985.
Moritz, Charles, ed. "Stephen King." <u>Contemporary</u>
<u>Biography Yearbook 1981</u>. New York: H. H.
Wilson, 1981. 252-255.
Murphy. Michael J. <u>The Celluloid Vampires: A His-</u>
<u>tory and Filmography, 1897-1979</u>. Ann Arbor
MI: Pierian Press, 1979.
Patrouch, Joseph F. "Stephen King in Context." In
<u>Patterns of the Fantastic</u>. Ed. Donald M. Has-
sler. Mercer Island WA: Starmont House, 1983.
Philtrum Press publicity sheet for <u>The Eyes of the</u>
<u>Dragon</u>.
Pronzini, Bill. "Introduction." In <u>Werewolf! A</u>
<u>Chrestomathy of Lycanthropy</u>. Ed. Bill Pron-

zini. New York: Arbor House, 1979. xiii-xviii
[Book Club edition].

Rabkin, Eric S. "The Sources of the Fantastic." In
Fantastic Worlds: Myths, Tales, and Stories.
Ed. Eric S. Rabkin. New York: Oxford University Press, 1979. 27-39.

Ryan, Alan. "The Marsten House in 'Salem's Lot."
In Fear Itself. Eds. Tim Underwood and Chuck
Miller. New York: NAL/Plume, 1984: 187-198.

Schneider, Peter. "Collecting the Works of Stephen
King." AB Bookman's Weekly. 24 October 1983:
2709-2711.

Schweitzer, Darrell, ed. Discovering Modern Horror
Fiction I. Mercer Island WA: Starmont House,
1985.

--------- Discovering Stephen King. Mercer Island
WA: Starmont House, 1985.

Sherman, David. Review of Cycle of the Werewolf.
Fangoria 35 (April 1984): 37.

Slung, Michelle. "In the Matter of Stephen King."
Armchair Detective (Spring 1981): 147-149.

Small, Michael. "Peter Straub and Stephen King
Team Up for Fear." People 28 January 1985:
50-52.

Stamm, Michael. Review of Pet Sematary. Science
Fiction and Fantasy Book Review, 20 (December
1983): 35-36.

"Stephen King's Torrent of Horror." USA Today 11
July 1985.

Straub, Peter. "Meeting Stevie." In Fear Itself.
Eds. Tim Underwood and Chuck Miller. New
York NAL/Plume, 1984: 7-13.

Strouse, Jean. "Beware of the Dog." Newsweek 31
August 1981: 64. Review of Cujo.

Stump, Debra. "A Matter of Choice: King's Cujo and
Malamud's The Natural." In Discovering Stephen King. Ed. Darrell Schweitzer. Mercer
Island WA: Starmont House, 1985. 131-140.

Thompson, Andrea. "The Thrills, Chills, and Skills
of Stephen King." McCalls (February 1983):
74-75.

Tolkien, J. R. R. "On Fairy-Stories." In The Tolkien Reader. New York: Ballantine, 1966.
Rpt. of Oxford University Press, 1947.

Underwood, Tim and Chuck Miller. Fear Itself: The
Horror Fiction of Stephen King. San Francisco
CA: Underwood-Miller, 1982; New York: NAL/
Plume, 1984.

Van Hise, James, ed. _Enterprise Incidents Presents Stephen King_. Tampa FL: New Media Publishing, 1984.

Warner Brothers publicity blurb. _Cujo_ videocassette, 1984.

Warren, Alan. "Has Success Spoiled Stephen King?" In _Discovering Stephen King_. Ed. Darrell Schweitzer. Mercer Island WA: Starmont House, 1985. 15-25.

Wiater, Stanley and Roger Anker. "Horror Partners." _Fangoria_, No. 42 (1985): 10-13.

Winter, Douglas E. "The Reader's Guide to Stephen King." Mercer Island WA: Starmont House, 1982.

---------- _Stephen King: The Art of Darkness_. New York: NAL, 1984

---------- "Stephen King, Peter Straub, & the Quest for _The Talisman_." _Twilight Zone Magazine_ (January/February 1985).

Yarbro, Chelsea Quinn. "Cinderella's Revenge: Twists on Fairy Tale and Mythic Themes in the Works of Stephen King." In _Fear Itself_. Eds. Tim Underwood and Chuck Miller. New York: NAL/Plume, 1984. 63-74.

SELECTIVE INDEX OF NAMES AND TITLES

(Excluding references to works mentioned in the "Checklist" and "List of Works Cited" sections)

189

www.ingramcontent.com/pod-product-compliance
Lightning Source LLC
La Vergne TN
LVHW011229080426
835509LV00005B/392